# ACTS

## (chapters 15–28)
## An Irrepressible Witness

**PROJECT DIRECTOR:**
James F. Couch, Jr.

**WRITING & EDITORIAL TEAM:**
Keith Madsen, Cathy Tardif, Katy Harris

**PRODUCTION TEAM:**
Sharon Penington, Erika Tiepel

SERENDIPITY HOUSE • Nashville, TN

Published by Serendipity House Publisher
Littleton, Colorado

International Standard Book Number: 1-57494-093-7

ACKNOWLEDGMENTS

To Zondervan Bible Publishers
for permission to use
the NIV text,
*The Holy Bible, New International Bible Society.*
© 1973, 1978, 1984 by International Bible Society.
Used by permission of Zondervan Bible Publishers.

03  04  05  06  07 / 10  9  8  7  6  5  4  3  2

Serendipity House
1-800-525-9563 / www.serendipityhouse.com

# ACTS

## An Irrepressible Witness
### Acts 15–28

# Group Directory

**Pass this Directory around and have your Group Members
fill in their names and phone numbers**

| Name | Phone |
|------|-------|
| _____ | _____ |
| _____ | _____ |
| _____ | _____ |
| _____ | _____ |
| _____ | _____ |
| _____ | _____ |
| _____ | _____ |
| _____ | _____ |
| _____ | _____ |
| _____ | _____ |
| _____ | _____ |
| _____ | _____ |
| _____ | _____ |
| _____ | _____ |

# TABLE OF CONTENTS

# CORE VALUES

**Community:** The purpose of this curriculum is to build community within the body of believers around Jesus Christ.

**Group Process:** To build community, the curriculum must be designed to take a group through a step-by-step process of sharing your story with one another.

**Interactive Bible Study:** To share your "story," the approach to Scripture in the curriculum needs to be open-ended and right brain—to "level the playing field" and encourage everyone to share.

**Developmental Stages:** To provide a healthy program throughout the four stages of the life cycle of a group, the curriculum needs to offer courses on three levels of commitment: (1) Beginner Level—low-level entry, high structure, to level the playing field; (2) Growth Level—deeper Bible study, flexible structure, to encourage group accountability; (3) Discipleship Level—in-depth Bible study, open structure, to move the group into high gear.

**Target Audiences:** To build community throughout the culture of the church, the curriculum needs to be flexible, adaptable and transferable into the structure of the average church.

# INTRODUCTION

Each healthy small group will move through various stages as it matures.

**Growth Stage:** Here the group begins to care for one another as it learns to apply what they learn through Bible study, worship and prayer.

**Develop Stage:** The inductive Bible study deepens while the group members discover and develop gifts and skills. The group explores ways to invite their neighbors and coworkers to group meetings.

**Birth Stage:** This is the time in which group members form relationships and begin to develop community. The group will spend more time in ice-breaker exercises, relational Bible study and covenant building.

**Multiply Stage:** The group begins the multiplication process. Members pray about their involvement in new groups. The "new" groups begin the lifecycle again with the Birth Stage.

**Subgrouping:** If you have nine or more people at a meeting, Serendipity recommends you divide into subgroups of 3–6 for the Bible study. Ask one person to be the leader of each subgroup and to follow the directions for the Bible study. After 30 minutes, the Group Leader will call "time" and ask all subgroups to come together for the Caring Time.

Each group meeting should include all parts of the "three-part agenda."

**Ice-Breaker:** Fun, history-giving questions are designed to warm the group and to build understanding about the other group members. You can choose to use all of the Ice-Breaker questions, especially if there is a new group member that will need help in feeling comfortable with the group.

**Bible Study:** The heart of each meeting is the reading and examination of the Bible. The questions are open, discover questions that lead to further inquiry. Reference notes are provided to give everyone a "level playing field." The emphasis is on understanding what the Bible says and applying the truth to real life. The questions for each session build. There is always at least one "going deeper" question provided. You should always leave time for the last of the "questions for interaction." Should you choose, you can use the optional "going deeper" question to satisfy the desire for the challenging questions in groups that have been together for a while.

**Caring Time:** All study should point us to actions. Each session ends with prayer and direction in caring for the needs of the group members. You can choose between several questions. You should always pray for the "empty chair." Who do you know that could fill that void in your group?

**Sharing Your Story:** These sessions are designed for members to share a little of their personal lives each time. Through a number of special techniques each member is encouraged to move from low risk less personal sharing to higher risk responses. This helps develop the sense of community and facilitates care giving.

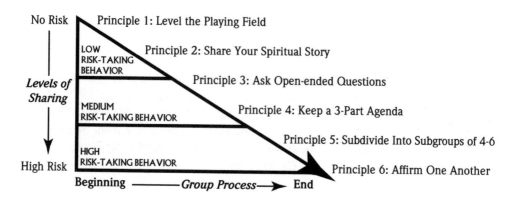

**Group Covenant:** A group covenant is a "contract" that spells out your expectations and the ground rules for your group. It's very important that your group discuss these issues—preferably as part of the first session.

GROUND RULES:

- *Priority:* While you are in the group, you give the group meeting priority.

- *Participation:* Everyone participates and no one dominates.

- *Respect:* Everyone is given the right to their own opinion and all questions are encouraged and respected.

- *Confidentiality:* Anything that is said in the meeting is never repeated outside the meeting.

- *Empty Chair:* The group stays open to new people at every meeting.

- *Support:* Permission is given to call upon each other in time of need—even in the middle of the night.

- *Advice Giving:* Unsolicited advice is not allowed.

- *Mission:* We agree to do everything in our power to start a new group as our mission.

ISSUES:

- The time and place this group is going to meet is:_____

- Responsibility for refreshments is: _____

- Childcare is _____ responsibility.

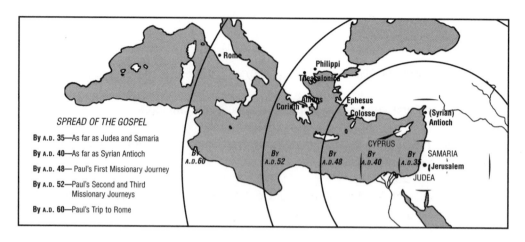

**SPREAD OF THE GOSPEL**

By A.D. 35—As far as Judea and Samaria

By A.D. 40—As far as Syrian Antioch

By A.D. 48—Paul's First Missionary Journey

By A.D. 52—Paul's Second and Third
Missionary Journeys

By A.D. 60—Paul's Trip to Rome

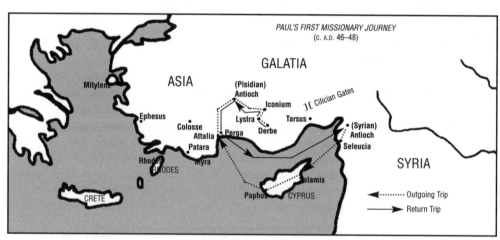

PAUL'S FIRST MISSIONARY JOURNEY
(C. A.D. 46–48)

⬅········ Outgoing Trip

⟶ Return Trip

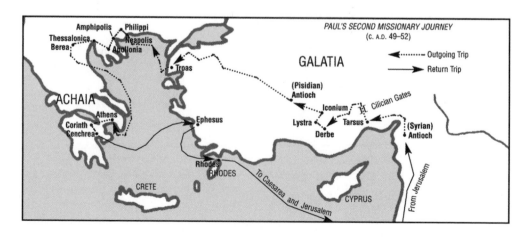

PAUL'S SECOND MISSIONARY JOURNEY
(C. A.D. 49–52)

⬅········ Outgoing Trip

⟶ Return Trip

# Session 1
# The Jerusalem Council

Scripture   Acts 15:1–21

## WELCOME

Welcome to this study of Acts, chapters 15–28! Together we will follow the exciting journeys of Peter, Paul and the rest of the disciples as they spread the Gospel and lead many to Christ. They face hardship and persecution along the way, but with the help of the Holy Spirit the church grows and prospers.

## ICE-BREAKER                                    15 Min.
### Connect with your Group

**Leader**

Be sure to read introductory material in the front of this book prior to the first session. To help your group members get acquainted, have each person introduce him or herself and then take turns answering one or two of the Ice-Breaker questions.

Today we are beginning a time of learning, sharing and growing together. Take some time to get to know one another by sharing your responses to the following questions.

1.  What most frequently caused disputes in the family in which you were raised?

2.  When it comes to handling disputes, what is your style most likely to be?
    ❏ Yelling and stomping around.
    ❏ Verbal volleys of blame and sarcasm.
    ❏ Calmly talking it out.
    ❏ Ignoring the issue altogether.
    ❏ Other _____.

3.  What church dispute has disturbed you the most?

# BIBLE STUDY 30 Min.
## READ SCRIPTURE AND DISCUSS

**LEADER**

Ask three members of the group, selected ahead of time, to read aloud the passage. Have one member read Luke's narration; another read the part of Peter; and the other read the part of James. Then discuss the questions that follow, dividing into subgroups of four or five as necessary. Be sure to save at least 15 minutes for the Caring Time.

Today we find the early church faced with resolving a conflict among the believers. Read Acts 15:1–21 and see how the Holy Spirit gives Peter and James wisdom in dealing with this matter of Christian Gentiles having to follow Jewish customs.

## The Church Meets in Jerusalem

Luke: **15** *Some men came down from Judea to Antioch and were teaching the brothers: "Unless you are circumcised, according to the custom taught by Moses, you cannot be saved." ²This brought Paul and Barnabas into sharp dispute and debate with them. So Paul and Barnabas were appointed, along with some other believers, to go up to Jerusalem to see the apostles and elders about this question.... ⁴When they came to Jerusalem, they were welcomed by the church and the apostles and elders, to whom they reported everything God had done through them. ⁵Then some of the believers who belonged to the party of the Pharisees stood up and said, "The Gentiles must be circumcised and required to obey the law of Moses." ⁶The apostles and elders met to consider this question. ⁷After much discussion, Peter got up and addressed them:*

Peter: *"Brothers, you know that some time ago God made a choice among you that the Gentiles might hear from my lips the message of the gospel and believe. ⁸God, who knows the heart, showed that he accepted them by giving the Holy Spirit to them, just as he did to us. ⁹He made no distinction between us and them, for he purified their hearts by faith. ¹⁰Now then, why do you try to test God by putting on the necks of the disciples a yoke that neither we nor our fathers have been able to bear? ¹¹No! We believe it is through the grace of our Lord Jesus that we are saved, just as they are."*

Luke: *¹²The whole assembly became silent as they listened to Barnabas and Paul telling about the miraculous signs and wonders God had done among the Gentiles through them. ¹³When they finished, James spoke up:*

James: *"Brothers, listen to me. ¹⁴Simon has described to us how God at first showed his concern by taking from the Gentiles a people for himself. ... ¹⁹"It is my judgment, therefore, that we should not make it difficult for the Gentiles who are turning to God. ²⁰Instead we should write to them, telling them to abstain from food polluted by idols, from sexual immorality, from the meat of strangled animals and from blood. ²¹For Moses has been preached in every city from the earliest times and is read in the synagogues on every Sabbath."*

*Acts 15:1–21*

## QUESTIONS FOR INTERACTION

**LEADER**

Refer to the Summary and Study Notes at the end of this session. If 30 minutes is not enough time to answer all of the questions in this section, conclude the Bible Study by answering question #7.

1.  What is most likely to cause "sharp disputes" in your church today?
    ❐ Theological issues, like how to apply Scripture.
    ❐ Worship music disputes, like guitars vs. organ.
    ❐ Personality issues, like "pro-pastor" vs. "anti-pastor".
    ❐ Other _____.

2.  What do you see as the motivation of the "men from Judea" for causing this dispute?

3.  Who seem to be the authorities before whom this dispute is going to be argued?

4.  What does Peter say is the sign by which he knew that Gentile converts had been accepted (v. 8)?

5.  How are all people saved, according to Peter (v. 11)?

6.  From what are Gentile believers to abstain, according to the agreement reached?

7.  What legalistic expectations do you sometimes find yourself trying to impose on others? What does this story say to you about such efforts?

**GOING DEEPER:** *If your group has time and/or wants a challenge, go on to this question.*

8.  How should the church today go about deciding what traditions can be discarded and which ones should be made binding on everyone in the church?

# CARING TIME                    15 Min.

## Apply the Lesson and Pray for One Another

## LEADER

Take some extra time in this first session to go over the introductory material at the front of this book. At the close, pass around your books and have everyone sign the Group Directory inside the front cover.

This very important time is for developing and expressing your concern for each other as group members by praying for one another.

**1.** Agree on the group covenant and ground rules which are described in the introduction to this book.

**2.** Begin the prayer time by taking turns and completing the following sentence: "My biggest concern or conflict right now is ..."

**3.** Share any other prayer requests and then close in prayer. Pray specifically for God to lead you to someone to bring next week to fill the empty chair.

---

### NEXT WEEK

Today we saw how the early church handled a conflict that still exists today. This conflict involves the role that the believer plays in his or her salvation. Peter reminded us that we are saved by grace alone, but James added that the Christian's life should reflect that grace with moral living. In the coming week, at the end of each day, consider how your words and actions reflected God's grace to others. Next week we will see the exciting spread of Christianity in Europe and the importance of following the leading of the Holy Spirit.

# NOTES ON ACTS 15:1–21

**Summary:** With the growing mission to the Gentiles, especially through the work of Paul and his missionary team, a conflict also grew. Should the Gentile converts be required to perform the ritual acts of the law that Jews had been required to do for centuries, particularly circumcision of males? In part, this controversy came about because this was a time of less differentiation between Christian and Jew. Those Jews who believed in Christ did not think they had converted to a new religion— they believed they had found the one their faith had been looking to for some time. As a result, they still held to many of the Jewish ways. Paul and his Gentile converts saw no need for this, since Paul taught that Jesus brought freedom from the old Jewish law.

To address this controversy, all the leaders of the church met together in what has since come to be known as the First Church Council. In the centuries to come there would be a number of such councils convened in order to decide on matters of correct doctrine in the face of ideas that were thought to be heretical. It was out of such councils that came what we know today as the Nicene Creed and the Apostles' Creed.

In this particular council the item of contention was the circumcision of Gentiles. While this council made a decision against requiring circumcision, it didn't entirely solve the problem between Gentile and Jewish Christians. In Paul's letter to the Galatians, written after these events, we read that the conflict persisted, and that even Peter vacillated on the issue (Gal. 2:11–14). However, by making this decision the church had something to which they could refer in mediating these conflicts. For the future of the church this was a vital direction, because it made possible a much more open fellowship in which Gentiles could participate without cultural restraints. This critical meeting of the church marked its first self-conscious departure from orthodox Judaism. Had the council decided to support the claims of the Jewish believers, Christianity would have remained only another sect within Judaism.

**15:1–4** The controversy surrounding circumcision stirred up such a debate that the church felt it necessary to call together the recognized leaders from Jerusalem and Antioch to settle the issue. This is considered to be the First Church Council.

**15:5 *the believers who belonged to the party of the Pharisees.*** The resistance to allowing Gentiles into the church originated with Jewish Christians who had formerly been Pharisees. This small but influential sect was widely respected for its adherence to the Old Testament Law and traditions. Their concern arose from a genuine desire to insure that God's honor was not violated through disregard of his Law. To

them, the offer of the Gospel apart from the Law was inconceivable since for centuries their people had been taught to look to the Law to discern God's will. Paul's ministry seemed like a slap in Israel's face—an unthinkable rejection of all the covenant responsibilities of God's chosen people. That Christians could also think of themselves as Pharisees again shows that the people of the time hadn't seen themselves as joining a new religion when they became followers of Christ. They retained their allegiance to the Jewish sect that they had been part of previously. Remember, the Pharisees believed in all of the books we count as the Hebrew Scriptures (in contrast to the Sadducees who only believed in the first five books of the Old Testament), and they believed in angels and life after death. Therefore, even though Jesus had many conflicts with Pharisees over their extreme emphasis on adherence to the Law, the Pharisees still had many beliefs in common with Jesus.

**15:7 *Peter got up and addressed them.*** Peter's point was that down through history the Jewish people had failed miserably in living up to the Law. Why then impose it on the Gentiles? His words here are reminiscent of Jesus' words in Luke 11:46, where he said, "And you experts in the law, woe to you, because you load people down with burdens they can hardly carry, and you yourselves will not lift one finger to help them." The direction for the future needed to be one of grace. Sure, God still expected moral behavior from people. He was not eliminating the role of moral laws (although Jesus simplified them by saying they were summed up in essentially two commandments: love God with all your heart, mind and soul; and love your neighbor as yourself). Rather, he was saying that legalism was a burden that none of us need to bear. We should love as he commanded, and then rely on God's grace and forgiveness when we fall short. ***the Gentiles might hear from my lips.*** As part of the discussion, Peter recounts his experience with Cornelius, which may have occurred 10 or more years earlier (10:1–11:18). The fact that Cornelius experienced the presence of the Spirit in the same way the disciples did was proof to him that God accepted the Gentiles quite apart from the practice of Jewish law.

**15:9–11** It is by faith in Jesus that one is made pure by God. The fact that it *has* to be that way is made plain by the fact that neither Israel as a nation nor any Jew as an individual ever managed to live up to all the demands of the Law. This affirmation of God's intent to save Gentiles through faith in Jesus is Peter's last statement in Acts.

**15:13–21** James was the leader of the Jerusalem church, and the ultimate decision as to the position of the Jerusalem church was his to make. Since in Galatians 2:11–13 James appears to have represented those who believed that Gentiles could not be considered equal members of the church with Jews, it may be that this council was the turning point when he realized the scope of Jesus' mission. James' affirmation of God's plan to save all types of people through faith in Jesus is his last statement in Acts as well.

**15:15 *The words of the prophets.*** James' quote is primarily rooted in the Septuagint version of Amos 9:11–12. The Old Testament books of Hosea through Malachi were contained on a single scroll. To quote one was to assume the support of the others.

**15:16–18** The original context of the prophecy was the anticipation of the destruction of Israel (722 B.C.) after which God would one day return the nation to its former glory as in David's day. James sees that the way God is rebuilding "David's ... tent" (a symbol of God's presence with Israel) is by establishing his church, made up of all types of people who seek God. The differences between the Septuagint version quoted here and what is found in our Old Testament are a result of adding a *d* to the Hebrew word *yiresu* (possessing) to obtain *yirdresu* (seeking), and a dispute about whether the Hebrew word *dm* should be vocalized as *Edom* (the name of a country south of Israel) or as *adam* (the Hebrew word for humanity). In either case, the point is that God's new people will include Gentiles as well as Jews.

**15:19 *It is my judgment, therefore.*** While some have seen Peter as "head" of the church at this point, it is James, the half-brother of Jesus, who actually seems to make the decision to not require circumcision. The rest of the church concurs, but the leadership seems to be James'.

**15:20** *telling them to abstain.* These considerations sum up the laws in Leviticus 17–27 that applied to Israel and all foreigners who lived within her borders. *food polluted by idols.* In Gentile areas meat was sold only after the animal had been sacrificed as part of a worship service to an idol. The eating of such food was later to be a source of controversy between Jewish and Gentile believers in Rome (Rom. 14:1–8) and Corinth (1 Cor. 8). *sexual immorality.* This may be related to "the pollution of idols" since idolatry sometimes involved ritual prostitution (1 Cor. 6:12–20). *meat of strangled animals and from blood.* Jews were forbidden to eat meat that had any blood in it (Lev. 17:10–14). Gentiles would make the sharing of meals with Jewish believers easier if they would respect this tradition.

# SESSION 2
# THE GOSPEL COMES TO EUROPE

SCRIPTURE ACTS 16:6–15

## LAST WEEK

The early church was not spared from conflict, as we discovered in last week's session. Led by the Holy Spirit, Peter and James decided that the Gentile Christians did not have to conform to all of the Jewish customs. They reminded the believers, along with us, that we are saved through the grace of Jesus, not by what customs or rules we might follow. This week we will again see the supernatural leading of the Holy Spirit in the missionary travels of Paul and his companions in Europe.

## ICE-BREAKER                                    15 Min.
### CONNECT WITH YOUR GROUP

**LEADER**

Begin the session with a word of prayer. Have your group members take turns sharing their responses to one, two or all three of the Ice-Breaker questions. Be sure that everyone gets a chance to participate.

The only thing that never changes is change! Get to know each other better by sharing how change has impacted your life.

1. When have unforeseen obstacles necessitated a change in plans for you?

2. How do you generally react when you have to make a change in plans (a long-planned vacation is delayed, rain cancels the picnic, etc.)?

3. When has a change in plans brought an unexpected "serendipity" to your life?

# BIBLE STUDY

## READ SCRIPTURE AND DISCUSS

# 30 Min.

**LEADER**

Have a member of the group, selected ahead of time to read aloud the passage. (Someone who doesn't mind trying difficult words!) Then divide into subgroups of four or five and discuss the Questions for Interaction.

Read Acts 16:6–15 about the missionary travels of Paul and his fellow believers. Note the role of the Holy Spirit in guiding their paths.

## Called to Macedonia

*⁶Paul and his companions traveled throughout the region of Phrygia and Galatia, having been kept by the Holy Spirit from preaching the word in the province of Asia. ⁷When they came to the border of Mysia, they tried to enter Bithynia, but the Spirit of Jesus would not allow them to. ⁸So they passed by Mysia and went down to Troas. ⁹During the night Paul had a vision of a man of Macedonia standing and begging him, "Come over to Macedonia and help us." ¹⁰After Paul had seen the vision, we got ready at once to leave for Macedonia, concluding that God had called us to preach the gospel to them.*

*¹¹From Troas we put out to sea and sailed straight for Samothrace, and the next day on to Neapolis. ¹²From there we traveled to Philippi, a Roman colony and the leading city of that district of Macedonia. And we stayed there several days.*

*¹³On the Sabbath we went outside the city gate to the river, where we expected to find a place of prayer. We sat down and began to speak to the women who had gathered there. ¹⁴One of those listening was a woman named Lydia, a dealer in purple cloth from the city of Thyatira, who was a worshiper of God. The Lord opened her heart to respond to Paul's message. ¹⁵When she and the members of her household were baptized, she invited us to her home. "If you consider me a believer in the Lord," she said, "come and stay at my house." And she persuaded us.*

*Acts 16:6–15*

Faith was counted as Rigeousness – Aberahams bosom.
Acts 2: power Anointing

**LEADER**

Refer to the Summary and Study Notes at the end of this session as needed. If 30 minutes is not enough time to answer all of the questions in this section, conclude the Bible Study by answering question #7.

## QUESTIONS FOR INTERACTION

**1.** If you had dreamed about the man in Macedonia, how would you have most likely reacted?
❒ Figured it was something you ate.
❒ Dismissed it as a dream.
❒ Considered it a message from God.
❒ Other _____.

Jn 20 - Upper room - rose again - showed wounds
He breathed on then as an act of transfering
power unto life

2. What events may Paul have interpreted as meaning that the Holy Spirit or Spirit of Christ did not want him going into Asia or Bithynia? What vision redirected his path?

3. Who seems to have been the first convert in Europe?

4. What business did this convert have, and why was it particularly lucrative (see note on v. 14)?

5. What gave Paul such a strong sensitivity to the Holy Spirit's guidance?

   *Full time ministry - Always listening*

6. What obstacles do you see ahead of you in your present life path? Are these obstacles just normal obstacles that come to life, or are they God's way of telling you to take another direction? How can you tell?

   *All obsticals should have a bearing on your relatinship w/GOD*
   *Allso ways should be effected by Goos relatonship w/ you*

7. What do you need to do to open yourself up more to the guidance of the Holy Spirit?
   □ Study Scripture more.
   □ Pray more.
   □ Other _____.

   *Epe 4: Paradise closed / Heaven open*
   *It is finished*

   **GOING DEEPER:** *If your group has time and/or wants a challenge, go on to this question.*

   *Abrahams busum - paradise*

8. Had Paul *not* been sensitive to the Spirit's guidance, how would it have affected the conversion of Lydia in particular and Europe in general? Would God have just found another way?

   *Baptism of repentance - John baptised people for sin*
   *John was concieved w/ the holy spint. (prepared - make way)*
   *40 - preparation Jesus was [washed] as a preist - to follow the whole law - fullfilling*
   *scripture*
   *∆ GOD's busiten - Decipeling*
   *∆ Nurishing*
   *∆ Replenthshing*
   *∆ God Restores*
   *∝ marrage was inshituted before sin*
   *∙ Created to be a blesing - when sin comsin it fails.*
   *EPE4 - Keys + saints from Hates to Heaven. Capt us Free* **21**

# CARING TIME                          15 Min.

## APPLY THE LESSON AND PRAY FOR ONE ANOTHER

**LEADER**

Bring the group members back together for the Caring Time. Begin by sharing responses to all three questions. Then share prayer requests and close in a group prayer. Those who do not feel comfortable praying out loud should not feel pressured to do so. As the leader, conclude the prayer time and be sure to pray for the empty chair.

Take time now to share how the Holy Spirit is working in your life and to pray for one another and support one another.

**1.** How is your relationship with Jesus right now?
- ❒ Close.
- ❒ Distant.
- ❒ Improving.
- ❒ Strained.
- ❒ Other _____.

**2.** What is something you feel God may be calling you to do?

**3.** Have each member of the group finish the sentence: "Right now I am seeking the guidance of the Holy Spirit to ...." Then pray for these needs for guidance.

## NEXT WEEK

Today we saw a dramatic example of the work of the Holy Spirit in the early church. That same Holy Spirit is with us today and can work just as dramatically in our lives. In the coming week, pray daily that you will be open to the leading of the Holy Spirit. Next week we will again see the power of God at work when Paul and Silas are miraculously freed from prison. But that's not the end of the story. Paul and Silas use this incredible situation to bring salvation to the jailer and his family.

# NOTES on Acts 16:6–15

**Summary:** One of the most obvious facts about the work of the church in Acts is that the Holy Spirit was an integral part of all that happened. The Holy Spirit is referred to no less than 41 times in the book. Certainly most of us remember that the Holy Spirit filled the disciples at Pentecost (ch. 2). The Holy Spirit also helped Peter when he was hauled before the Sanhedrin (4:8); filled Stephen in his hour of martyrdom (7:55); healed Saul's (Paul's) blindness (9:17–19); brought increased numbers to the church (9:31); led Gentiles to become believers (10:44–48); set apart Paul and Barnabas for their missionary journeys (13:2); and prepared Paul for the suffering he would face (20:23).

In our passage for this week, the apostle Paul shows a special sensitivity to the Holy Spirit's leading, and as a result he takes the Gospel to Europe for the first time. How significant this is! It was in Europe that the Gospel grew and spread throughout the rest of the earth. Because it became the dominant faith in Europe, it came to America and became the dominant faith here as well.

The events of this chapter occur in what is called Paul's second missionary journey. The Holy Spirit led the missionary team, and that leading was away from Asia and Bithynia. In essence, they were told not to divert their path to the right or the left, but to go straight ahead, which would have been the direction of Europe. When they got to Troas, which is on the Aegean Sea across from Greece, Paul saw a vision at night. It was a man of Macedonia, calling them to "come over and help us." Macedonia is part of Greece. Right away Paul knew that this was why they had been forbidden to go in the direction he had considered. He did not hesitate to follow what he believed to be the call of the Holy Spirit. Our text tells us "we got ready at once to leave for Macedonia" (v. 10).

As a result of following the guidance of the Holy Spirit, a wealthy woman (Lydia) was converted who became a valuable supporter of Christ; and a church was started at Philippi that became one of Paul's most loyal churches. The eventual result was the beginning of the church in Europe, which then spread throughout the world. What better commendation could there be for following the guidance of the Spirit?

**16:6–7 the Holy Spirit/the Spirit of Jesus.** Luke clearly identifies the ongoing work of Jesus with the agency of the Holy Spirit in the lives of the apostles.

**16:7 would not allow them to.** Why Jesus would not allow Paul and Silas to preach in Asia and Bithynia is not given. Later on, the apostle Peter was in contact with churches in that area so they were not left bereft of the Gospel (1 Peter 1:1).

**16:8 Troas.** An important seaport on the Aegean Sea. While it appears Paul did not do any evangelistic work here at this time, he did do so later on (2 Cor. 2:12).

**16:9 Macedonia.** This area of northern Greece had been the dominant power under Alexander the Great in the fourth century B.C.

**16:10 we.** Verses 10–17 is the first of four passages written in the first person

(20:5–21:18; 27:1–28:16), indicating that Luke himself was accompanying Paul at these points.

**16:11–12** In two days they arrived at Macedonia, landing at Neapolis. Philippi was a short distance to the west.

**16:12 *the leading city of that district.*** The Greek here is uncertain. Since Philippi was neither the largest city nor the capital of the province, it probably should read simply, "a city of the first district of Macedonia." Macedonia was a Roman province divided into four districts. Paul's later letter to the Philippians is one of his warmest, most positive letters, and it indicates that the church here was very supportive of him, even when other churches seemed to have forgotten about his needs (Phil. 4:15–16).

**16:13** Ten men were required in order to form a synagogue. The fact that there was no synagogue in Philippi indicates how small the Jewish population was. ***outside the city gate to the river.*** The Jews may have been forbidden to meet inside the city limits, or they may have wanted to be near a river to perform their ceremonial washings.

**16:14 *Lydia.*** Macedonian women enjoyed far more freedom and opportunities than many of their counterparts elsewhere. Lydia was a businesswoman involved in selling purple cloth, a luxury item indicating that she was a woman of wealth. ***Thyatira.*** A city in the province of Asia noted for its dyeing industry. These dyes were made by taking the glands of the myrax, a purple sea snail, and simmering them in pans for a few days. They then dipped cloth in it for a dye that would never fade. Purple was considered a kingly color, and there were laws in Rome that limited who could wear it. Evidence indicates that there was a Jewish community in Thyatira, which probably influenced Lydia toward faith in the God of the Jews. ***a worshiper of God.*** Lydia was referred to as "a worshiper of God." That meant that, while a Gentile, she worshiped the God of Abraham. She was not a full proselyte, possibly because she did not want to be bound by Jewish ceremonial law. Lydia demonstrated her faith in Jesus as the Messiah by baptism and by offering hospitality to the missionaries.

**16:15 *the members of her household.*** It was customary for children and servants to embrace the faith of their master or mistress (Acts 11:14).

# PAUL AND SILAS IN PRISON

SCRIPTURE ACTS 16:16–40

> **LAST WEEK**
>
> In last week's session we saw how the Holy Spirit led Paul and his companions to bring the Gospel to Europe. The establishment of the church in this region was a significant turning point for Christianity. Because it became the dominant faith in Europe, it came to America and eventually spread throughout the world. This week we will encounter the trials and triumphs of Paul and Silas as they face prison and suffering due to freeing a slave girl from an occult spirit of fortune-telling.

## ICE-BREAKER                    15 Min.
### CONNECT WITH YOUR GROUP

**LEADER**

Choose one or two of the Ice-Breaker questions. If you have a new group member you may want to do all three. Remember to stick closely to the three-part agenda and the time allowed for each segment.

Everyone who travels the road of life experiences both good times and bad. Take turns sharing how you have handled some of the "bumps" along the road of your life.

**1.** When have you been in an earthquake or other natural disaster? How did it affect you, and what, if anything, did you do to protect yourself?

**2.** When, if ever, have you had to go to court? What accusations were made against you? How fairly were you treated?

**3.** When do you remember having to "eat crow"? When do you remember getting someone else to "eat crow"? Did you "rub it in" or graciously let it pass?

# BIBLE STUDY 30 Min.
## READ SCRIPTURE AND DISCUSS

**LEADER**

Have a member of the group, selected ahead of time, read aloud the Scripture passage. Then discuss the Questions for Interaction, breaking up into smaller subgroups as necessary.

Today we see Paul and Silas encounter one of those unexpected "bumps" in life. After freeing a slave girl of an evil spirit, they find themselves stripped, severely flogged and put in stocks in prison. Read Acts 16:16–40 and note the miraculous ending to this story.

### Paul and Silas in Prison

*16Once when we were going to the place of prayer, we were met by a slave girl who had a spirit by which she predicted the future. She earned a great deal of money for her owners by fortune-telling. 17This girl followed Paul and the rest of us, shouting, "These men are servants of the Most High God, who are telling you the way to be saved." 18She kept this up for many days. Finally Paul became so troubled that he turned around and said to the spirit, "In the name of Jesus Christ I command you to come out of her!" At that moment the spirit left her.*

*19When the owners of the slave girl realized that their hope of making money was gone, they seized Paul and Silas and dragged them into the marketplace to face the authorities. 20They brought them before the magistrates and said, "These men are Jews, and are throwing our city into an uproar 21by advocating customs unlawful for us Romans to accept or practice."*

*22The crowd joined in the attack against Paul and Silas, and the magistrates ordered them to be stripped and beaten. 23After they had been severely flogged, they were thrown into prison, and the jailer was commanded to guard them carefully. 24Upon receiving such orders, he put them in the inner cell and fastened their feet in the stocks.*

*25About midnight Paul and Silas were praying and singing hymns to God, and the other prisoners were listening to them. 26Suddenly there was such a violent earthquake that the foundations of the prison were shaken. At once all the prison doors flew open, and everybody's chains came loose. 27The jailer woke up, and when he saw the prison doors open, he drew his sword and was about to kill himself because he thought the prisoners had escaped. 28But Paul shouted, "Don't harm yourself! We are all here!"*

*29The jailer called for lights, rushed in and fell trembling before Paul and Silas. 30He then brought them out and asked, "Sirs, what must I do to be saved?"*

*31They replied, "Believe in the Lord Jesus, and you will be saved—you and your household." 32Then they spoke the word of the Lord to him and to all the others in his house. 33At that hour of the night the jailer took them and washed their wounds; then immediately he and all his family were baptized.* <sup>34</sup>*The jailer brought them into his house and set a meal before them; he was filled with joy because he had come to believe in God—he and his whole family.*

<sup>35</sup>*When it was daylight, the magistrates sent their officers to the jailer with the order: "Release those men."* <sup>36</sup>*The jailer told Paul, "The magistrates have ordered that you and Silas be released. Now you can leave. Go in peace."*

<sup>37</sup>*But Paul said to the officers: "They beat us publicly without a trial, even though we are Roman citizens, and threw us into prison. And now do they want to get rid of us quietly? No! Let them come themselves and escort us out."*

<sup>38</sup>*The officers reported this to the magistrates, and when they heard that Paul and Silas were Roman citizens, they were alarmed.* <sup>39</sup>*They came to appease them and escorted them from the prison, requesting them to leave the city.* <sup>40</sup>*After Paul and Silas came out of the prison, they went to Lydia's house, where they met with the brothers and encouraged them. Then they left.*

*Acts 16:16–40*

## LEADER

Refer to the Summary and Study Notes at the end of this session as needed. If 30 minutes is not enough time to answer all of the questions in this section, conclude the Bible Study by answering question #8.

## QUESTIONS FOR INTERACTION

**1.** When in your life have you had a pest follow you around? What did this person do to bother you? How did you get rid of him or her?

**2.** What is the slave girl doing that bothers Paul? Why is this so disturbing to him?

**3.** Why are the owners of the slave girl upset that Paul has cast this evil spirit out of her? How do their accusations against him in court compare to what it was that really upset them?

**4.** What happened to set Paul, Silas and the others free from their chains? Why didn't they all just leave at that point?

**5.** Why does the jailer consider killing himself (see note on v. 27)? When he finds that all the prisoners are still there, why does he then seek the way to salvation?

**6.** Why does Paul refuse to leave at first when the magistrates order them released? What more is he asking for? Is this maneuver to salve his own ego, to benefit the mission or a little of both?

**7.** With whom in this story do you identify most strongly at this point of your life?

❏ The girl, who was abused and taken advantage of.
❏ Paul and Silas, imprisoned unjustly.
❏ The jailer, feeling frightened and like a failure, but seeking God.
❏ The jailer after being baptized, full of joy for what God has done.
❏ Paul and Silas, seeking apologies for the way you've been treated.
❏ Other _____.

**8.** From what "prison" has God released you? Because of your "prison" experience, whom can you now encourage (v. 40)?

**GOING DEEPER:** *If your group has time and/or wants a challenge, go on to this question.*

**9.** What precautions should a Christian businessperson take to make sure that he or she isn't taking advantage of employees, as the owners of this slave girl were? What should such a businessperson do if what is good for the employee turns out to be bad for business?

## CARING TIME                                    15 Min.
### APPLY THE LESSON AND PRAY FOR ONE ANOTHER

**LEADER**

Begin the Caring Time by having group members take turns sharing responses to all three questions. Be sure to save at least the last five minutes for a time of group prayer.

Following the example of Paul and Silas in verse 40, encourage one another with this time of sharing concerns and praying.

**1.** What miracle do you need in your life right now? How would that miracle be a blessing to others?

**2.** What fills you with joy when you think of all God has done for you?

**3.** On a scale of 1 to 10, how closely have you been walking with Jesus this week (1 being I have been running in the opposite direct and 10 being we are in lock step and having a great time)? What can this group do to help you in your walk?

## NEXT WEEK

Today we were reminded of the power of God, and how he can use even the most negative circumstances for good. We just need to keep our eyes on him and stay focused on our mission, as Paul and Silas did. In the coming week, resolve to spend some time alone with Jesus every day, away from the distractions of the world. Next week we will watch Paul discuss his beliefs with the philosophers in Athens and learn some effective techniques for sharing the Gospel.

# NOTES ON ACTS 16:16–40

**Summary:** Throughout history Christians have spent a lot of time in prison. For most people time in prison is "dead" time, full of despair, but Christians have used it to spread the Gospel. Some of this ministry has been done by letter writing. Paul wrote a number of his letters, including Philippians and Ephesians, from prison. In recent history, Dietrich Bonhoeffer wrote *Letters and Papers from Prison* and Martin Luther King, Jr. wrote *Letters from a Birmingham Jail.* In addition to this letter writing, others have testified to their jailers and to fellow inmates while in prison.

**16:17** *the way to be saved*. For Gentile pagans, this would mean deliverance from the powers of fate and impersonal forces.

**16:18** While what the girl said was true, the spirit that motivated her was not one Paul desired as a collaborator in his mission. Undoubtedly, it attracted attention but made Paul and Silas appear more as magicians than as representatives of God. Thus, Paul commanded the spirit to leave her.

**16:19** *their hope of making money was gone.* Luke adds a touch of irony by using the same verb here as he did in verse 18 to describe the departure of the spirit. The girl's worth to her masters was only in her gift of fortune-telling. As far as they were concerned, Paul had not delivered a girl from the power of evil, but had violated their property rights. *seized Paul and Silas.* The fact that Paul and Silas were seized while Luke and Timothy were not may be due to the racial prejudice against Jews that is more clearly seen in verse 20. *authorities.* These were two magistrates elected annually who held session in the public square. Excavations that date back to the second century show that the jail bordered the square.

**16:20** The charges do not refer to the owners' economic loss, but focus on two assertions sure to create public opposition: first, the men were creating a public disturbance; and second, they were advocating illegal actions against the state. Any public attention to the missionaries was caused by the slave girl's strange pronouncements, not their own actions. The second charge rests on the fact that Roman citizens were not to practice any religion forbidden by the state. Although this law was rarely enforced, its usefulness lay in allowing Rome the opportunity to crush any extremist groups that threatened Roman authority.

**16:22 *stripped and beaten.*** The authorities should have put Paul and Silas in custody to be formally tried; but pressured by the crowds, they publicly beat them without trial. Flogging was a severe punishment, as the victim was whipped by a rod that the magistrates carried as a symbol of their judicial authority to exercise judgment.

**16:24 *he put them in the inner cell and fastened their feet in the stocks.*** Why these prisoners were considered worthy of such precautions is uncertain, but it sets up a contrast with God's ability to free them in spite of the security measures taken to oppress them. The reader is to imagine Paul and Silas, backs badly bruised, crippled by stocks, locked away in a dark cell.

**16:25** The contrast between their attitude and their situation is immense! In spite of their pain and humiliation, these prisoners were singing hymns and praying to God, bearing witness to the other prisoners. The Greek verb implies their fellow captors listened intently to Paul and Silas.

**16:26** Earthquakes are not uncommon in the area— what was notable about this one was its timing! ***the prison doors flew open.*** The elaborate security measures had no effect when God's time for deliverance had come.

**16:27 *The jailer ... was about to kill himself.*** The punishment for a guard who allowed his prisoners to escape was that which the prisoner was to have received. The jailer preferred sudden death by his own hand rather than going through the public humiliation of a trial and execution by the authorities. His action was interrupted by Paul's assurance that no one had escaped.

**16:29–30** The combined factors of the stories of Paul's preaching (vv. 17–18), their prayers while imprisoned, and the earthquake were enough to lead the jailer to acknowledge that Paul and Silas must be indeed God's agents. His question fits in with the report of the slave girl: he wanted to know how he might be spared the effects of divine anger.

**16:31 *Believe in the Lord Jesus, and you will be saved.*** Paul's response is summed up in this single phrase: deliverance from the power of evil and from divine judgment is given to those who entrust themselves to Jesus as their Lord. Jesus is the Savior to those who respond to him as Lord.

**16:33–34** The belief of the jailer was shown both by the fact that he washed the prisoners' wounds and was himself washed by the water of baptism. This was followed by a meal at which Paul may have led in the Lord's Supper.

**16:35–40** The magistrates simply wanted to expel Paul and Silas from town to avoid any further trouble. However, the missionaries refused to go without a personal apology from the magistrates for their breach of justice. This was not simply a matter of self-vindication nor a matter of insisting on the proper administration of justice, as deserved as these things were under the circumstances. It was especially important for the protection of the young church in Philippi, since Paul's claim to citizenship showed he was not interested in violating Roman customs as he had been charged (v. 21). By being escorted out of the prison by the magistrates, a signal would be communicated to the community at large that the charges had been false. As a result, the community would be more likely to leave the young church alone.

**16:37** While local magistrates could execute punishment upon troublemakers without a trial, this was never to be the case when it was a Roman citizen who was charged. Citizenship included the right to a trial for any accusations. Citizenship was conferred only upon those born in certain cities (as in Paul's case), or those who could afford a bribe to pay for the privilege (22:28). The magistrates had overlooked the possibility that these two Jews might be citizens. If Paul reported their action to a higher authority, they could be in danger of losing their office.

**16:39** The magistrates did what they could to appease Paul and Silas, but still asked them to leave the city to avoid any further commotions by the community. Since the next "we" section does not occur until Paul passes through Macedonia once again (20:5), Luke apparently was left behind to strengthen the young church and train its leaders.

# SESSION 4
# PAUL PREACHES IN ATHENS

SCRIPTURE   ACTS 17:16–34

**LAST WEEK**

Paul and Silas were faced with imprisonment and suffering in last week's passage. In spite of their extremely difficult circumstances, they continued to praise God and witness to others. Today we will continue to follow Paul's missionary path as he debates the philosophers in Athens.

## ICE-BREAKER                                    15 Min.
### CONNECT WITH YOUR GROUP

**LEADER**

Choose one, two or all three of the Ice-Breaker questions. Welcome and introduce new group members.

Everyday we are faced with hearing different viewpoints and opinions. Take turns sharing your experiences in dealing with the opinions of others.

**1.**   When you were in junior high, who were you most likely to get into an argument with? How did you generally fare in those arguments?

**2.**   Again in junior high, where was the place you and your friends most frequently gathered to talk things over?

**3.**   In the town or city you grew up in, what would you say were the "gods" of the town?

# BIBLE STUDY

### READ SCRIPTURE AND DISCUSS

## 30 Min.

## LEADER

Select two members of the class ahead of time to read aloud the passage. Have one read the part of Luke, the narrator, and the other read the part of Paul. Have the whole class read the part of the philosophers. Then divide into subgroups as needed for discussion of the Questions for Interaction.

The apostle Paul is well known for his boldness in speaking out. He challenges the philosophers of Athens as to why they worship so many different idols, instead of the one true God. Read Acts 17:16–34 and note the way Paul presents the Gospel.

## Paul Preaches in Athens

Luke:
*16While Paul was waiting for them in Athens, he was greatly distressed to see that the city was full of idols. 17So he reasoned in the synagogue with the Jews and the God-fearing Greeks, as well as in the marketplace day by day with those who happened to be there. 18A group of Epicurean and Stoic philosophers began to dispute with him. Some of them asked,*

Philosophers:
*"What is this babbler trying to say?" Others remarked, "He seems to be advocating foreign gods."*

Luke:
*They said this because Paul was preaching the good news about Jesus and the resurrection. 19Then they took him and brought him to a meeting of the Areopagus, where they said to him,*

Philosophers:
*"May we know what this new teaching is that you are presenting? 20You are bringing some strange ideas to our ears, and we want to know what they mean."*

Luke:
*21(All the Athenians and the foreigners who lived there spent their time doing nothing but talking about and listening to the latest ideas.) 22Paul then stood up in the meeting of the Areopagus and said:*

Paul:
*"Men of Athens! I see that in every way you are very religious. 23For as I walked around and looked carefully at your objects of worship, I even found an altar with this inscription: TO AN UNKNOWN GOD. Now what you worship as something unknown I am going to proclaim to you.*

*24"The God who made the world and everything in it is the Lord of heaven and earth and does not live in temples built by hands. ... 28'For in him we live and move and have our being.' As some of your own poets have said, 'We are his offspring.'*

*29"Therefore since we are God's offspring, we should not think that the divine being is like gold or silver or stone—an image made by man's design and skill. ³⁰In the past God overlooked such ignorance, but now he commands all people everywhere to repent. ³¹For he has set a day when he will judge the world with justice by the man he has appointed. He has given proof of this to all men by raising him from the dead."*

Luke:     ³²*When they heard about the resurrection of the dead, some of them sneered, but others said,*

Philosophers:   *"We want to hear you again on this subject."*

Luke:     ³³*At that, Paul left the Council. ³⁴A few men became followers of Paul and believed. Among them was Dionysius, a member of the Areopagus, also a woman named Damaris, and a number of others.*

*Acts 17:16–34*

## LEADER

Refer to the Summary and Study Notes at the end of this session. If 30 minutes is not enough time to answer all of the questions in this section, conclude the Bible Study by answering question #7.

## QUESTIONS FOR INTERACTION

**1.** What "greatly distressed" Paul when he was in Athens (v. 16)?

**2.** Where have you gone recently and found yourself shocked by your surroundings? How did your reaction compare to Paul's?

**3.** What do you think convinced these Athenians to give Paul a chance to speak in the Areopagus?

**4.** When in Athens, why do you think Paul referred to the sayings of Greek poets instead of quoting Old Testament prophecy?

**5.** What do you think was the most effective thing Paul did in Athens?
  ❏ Affirming the philosophers for their religious inclinations.
  ❏ Referring to the poets and thinkers of Greece.
  ❏ Showing the fallacy of worshiping gods made by hands.
  ❏ Boldly proclaiming the resurrection of the dead to those who were skeptical about it.
  ❏ Other _____.

**6.** What is the difference between being "religious" and being committed to the one true God? Why is it difficult for some people to move from being vaguely religious to such a commitment?

**7.** Where are you right now in terms of this story?
- ❏ Listening to all the ideas you can (v. 21).
- ❏ Seeking an "unknown god" (v. 23).
- ❏ On the trail of the true God (v. 27).
- ❏ Committed to the God who raised Jesus from the dead (vv. 30–31).

**GOING DEEPER:** *If your group has time and/or wants a challenge, go on to this question.*

**8.** In sharing your testimony with someone of another faith, what is the proper balance between acknowledging the insights of that faith (v. 28), and declaring the uniqueness of what Christ has done (v. 31)?

# CARING TIME                    15 Min.
## APPLY THE LESSON AND PRAY FOR ONE ANOTHER

**LEADER**

Be sure to save at least 15 minutes for this important time. After sharing responses to all three questions and asking for prayer requests, close in a time of group prayer.

Take some time now to encourage one another in your faith by discussing the following questions and sharing prayer requests.

**1.** How has God been at work in your life this past week?

**2.** What have you found helpful in sharing your faith with your family and friends?

**3.** What "idols" in your life tend to distract you from being fully committed to God?

### NEXT WEEK

In today's lesson we saw Paul boldly and wisely speak out for his faith, in spite of the attitude of the culture around him. The people of Athens believed in worshiping many gods, while he was advocating worshiping the one true God. In the coming week, renew your commitment to the one true God by spending some extra time in prayer and Bible study each day. Next week we will again see the boldness of the Christians in sharing their faith. We will also see how important a mentor can be in keeping us on the right path.

# NOTES ON ACTS 17:16–34

**Summary:** Christianity has always clashed in one way or another with the culture in which it has found itself. Jesus spoke of this in an indirect way when he said in John 15:19, "If you belonged to the world, it would love you as its own. As it is, you do not belong to the world, but I have chosen you out of the world. That is why the world hates you." Most Christians do at one time or another feel the pinch of being in conflict with the values and direction of the secular society in which they live. When we feel this way, how do we react? Looking at how the apostle Paul reacted when he felt like "a fish out of water" in the culture of Athens may help us in our consideration of this issue.

At various points Paul reacted in four different ways:

(1) When Paul encountered for himself what was happening in Athens, his first reaction was one of shock. Verse 16 tells us, "While Paul was waiting for them in Athens, he was greatly distressed to see that the city was full of idols." No doubt Paul did know in his mind that Athens would be like it was. What Paul experienced in Athens was the emotional impact of what he had previously known to be true—Athens was a city that worshiped many false gods.

(2) After his initial shock, Paul turned to a more positive reaction of affirming what was good. He told the Athenians, "I see that in every way you are very religious" (v. 22). He could have said, "I see that you are all superstitious idolaters," but he knew that a positive approach changes people.

(3) The next thing that Paul did was to speak to the Athenians in the language of their culture. He referred to their statue "to an unknown god" (v. 23) and to the teachings of their poets (v. 28). This helped the people know that Paul knew and respected the contributions of their culture. What Paul didn't do was talk to them about all the prophecies of Hebrew Scripture. It wouldn't have made sense to them and they wouldn't have respected the source of authority.

(4) While Paul adapted the form of his message to the culture of Athens, he did not compromise the message itself. He knew that apart from the resurrection of Jesus Christ, this new faith would have no reason for existence, and would have no meaning (1 Cor. 15:12–28).

**17:17** Paul preached not only in the synagogue at Athens, but also in their marketplace where, three centuries before, Socrates likewise debated with anyone who would listen.

**17:18** *Epicurean and Stoic philosophers.* Epicurus maintained that a tranquil life free from pain, passions and fears was the highest good for humanity. This could be achieved only by detaching oneself from indulgence and the cares of the world. The Epicureans were practical atheists in that they believed the gods had no interest in humanity and were unknowable. The Stoics had a pantheistic idea of god as the World-Soul. People were a spark of the divine; upon death, one's immortal soul would be absorbed into the divine spirit. The ideal life was one of virtue that refused to give in before the pressures of circumstances and of human passions. *this babbler.* Literally, "seed-picker." This is a derisive term stemming from the actions of a bird that picks up seeds wherever it can find them. To the philosophers, Paul seemed like someone who picked up scraps of ideas here and there and then had the audacity to try to teach others. **foreign gods ... Jesus and the resurrection.** Since the Greek word for Jesus sounds something like the Greek name for the goddess of health, and since the Greek word for salvation is also used to speak of physical healing, his listeners thought Paul was talking about two new gods— Health and Resurrection.

**17:19 *Areopagus.*** Athens was a free city within the Roman Empire so the Areopagus had legal and judicial authority over what went on in the city. It does not appear that Paul himself is on trial (as though he was accused of breaking any laws) as much as his message itself is being evaluated as to its credibility and worth.

**17:23 *TO AN UNKNOWN GOD.*** Other writers of the time speak of statues and altars in Athens raised to gods "both known and unknown." The implicit admission of ignorance about God provided Paul with a point of entry for sharing the Gospel.

**17:24** Paul asserts that God is both the world's Creator and Sovereign: he is not the uninterested or removed god of Greek philosophy. **does not live in temples.** Euripides, a Greek philosopher, recognized this when he wrote, "What house built by craftsman could enclose the ... divine within enfolding walls?"

**17:25 *he is not served by human hands.*** With this, the philosophers would also agree. Plato had written, "What advantage accrues to the gods from what they get from us?"

**17:26** The Athenians had a tradition that they were different from other people in that they had sprung up from the soil of Athens itself (they were unique among other Greeks in that they had no tradition of how their ancestors migrated into the area). Paul's point is that they, like all people, derive from God's creation of humanity.

**17:27** Challenging the Epicurean assumption that God was unknowable, Paul says that God is knowable by those who seek after him. While the Stoics would agree with the nearness of God, the ideas of his separateness from creation and that one could know God personally would challenge them.

**17:28** Paul supports his points by quoting two Greek authors, Epimenides and Aratus. Both are from works about Zeus, and both were interpreted by the Stoics to refer to the *Logos*, the supreme source of reason and order in the universe. These quotes indicate that he recognized God revealed truth about himself even through other religions and philosophies.

**17:30 *God overlooked such ignorance.*** This reflects the Old Testament notion that sins committed in ignorance are less culpable than those done in defiance.

**17:32–34** The converts included Dionysius, a member of the Athenian council. Nothing more is said in the New Testament about Athens, so it is unlikely that these believers established a church at the time.

# SESSION 5
# TEACHING IN EPHESUS

SCRIPTURE ACTS 18:18–28

**LAST WEEK**

In last week's session we saw Paul debate the philosophers in Athens and challenge them with a new way of thinking about God. Those who listened to Paul reacted in many different ways—some called him a "babbler" and sneered, some were interested but not convinced, and a few became believers. We will also encounter many different reactions to our faith, but we must persevere as Paul did. Today we will take a look at the early church in Ephesus and how Priscilla and Aquila taught and mentored Apollos.

## ICE-BREAKER                                    15 Min.
### CONNECT WITH YOUR GROUP

**LEADER**

If you have a new group member today, remember to do all three Ice-Breaker questions to help him or her get acquainted with everyone.

Parents, teachers, pastors, coaches, employers—each of us can probably name at least one or two significant people that have had a very positive influence on our life. Take turns sharing your thoughts on receiving help and instruction from others.

1. Who was your favorite teacher when you were in grade school? What did you learn from this teacher? What made him or her an effective teacher?

2. How difficult was it for you to take correction when you were in grade school? Did it matter if that correction came from a parent, another adult or a sibling? How difficult is it for you to take correction now?

3. What was most likely to be debated in the household in which you were raised?
   ❏ Who was to do which chore.
   ❏ What to watch on television.
   ❏ Who was superior—boys or girls.
   ❏ Other _____

# BIBLE STUDY

## READ SCRIPTURE AND DISCUSS

# 30 Min.

## LEADER

Have a member of the group, selected ahead of time, read aloud the Scripture passage. Then discuss the Questions for Interaction, dividing into smaller subgroups of four or five.

We see in today's Scripture passage that Paul is very busy traveling and spreading the Good News of Jesus to all who will listen. However, he still takes the time to encourage and strengthen the disciples (v. 23). Priscilla and Aquila, companions of Paul, also take on this role as they mentor Apollos, who was boldly speaking out for the Lord. Read Acts 18:18–28 and note how Apollos reacts to this mentoring.

## Teaching in Ephesus

*18Paul stayed on in Corinth for some time. Then he left the brothers and sailed for Syria, accompanied by Priscilla and Aquila. Before he sailed, he had his hair cut off at Cenchrea because of a vow he had taken. 19They arrived at Ephesus, where Paul left Priscilla and Aquila. He himself went into the synagogue and reasoned with the Jews. 20When they asked him to spend more time with them, he declined. 21But as he left, he promised, "I will come back if it is God's will." Then he set sail from Ephesus. 22When he landed at Caesarea, he went up and greeted the church and then went down to Antioch.*

*23After spending some time in Antioch, Paul set out from there and traveled from place to place throughout the region of Galatia and Phrygia, strengthening all the disciples.*

*24Meanwhile a Jew named Apollos, a native of Alexandria, came to Ephesus. He was a learned man, with a thorough knowledge of the Scriptures. 25He had been instructed in the way of the Lord, and he spoke with great fervor and taught about Jesus accurately, though he knew only the baptism of John. 26He began to speak boldly in the synagogue. When Priscilla and Aquila heard him, they invited him to their home and explained to him the way of God more adequately.*

*27When Apollos wanted to go to Achaia, the brothers encouraged him and wrote to the disciples there to welcome him. On arriving, he was a great help to those who by grace had believed. 28For he vigorously refuted the Jews in public debate, proving from the Scriptures that Jesus was the Christ.*

*Acts 18:18–28*

## QUESTIONS FOR INTERACTION

1. When was the last time you had such a good time talking to a group of people that you immediately made plans to go back and see them again? Did you follow through with those plans?

2. How is Paul's reception by the Jews of Ephesus both similar to and different from his reception by the Jews of other cities (see vv. 19–21; 19:8–9; compare to 13:44–47; 14:2–6; 17:2–8,13–15)?

3. What was the main purpose of Paul's trip through Galatia and Phrygia (v. 23)? Why was such work so necessary?

4. What were the strengths of Apollos? What was his main shortcoming? Why did this shortcoming need to be corrected?

5. Who took Apollos aside and "explained to him the way of God more adequately" (v. 26)? What kind of qualities would these people need to have in order to correct the understanding of such a learned man?

6. Who more than anyone else has taken your own misunderstandings and "explained the way of God more adequately" to you? Was the process easy or difficult for you? For them?

7. If you could have a "Priscilla and Aquila" come to you right now and help you find a fuller understanding of God, what would those persons need to be like in order to help you? What areas of theological confusion would you like them to help you with?

**GOING DEEPER:** *If your group has time and/or wants a challenge, go on to this next question.*

8. What could you say in a public debate that would "prove" (or at least strongly support) your view that Jesus was the Christ, a unique messenger of God (v. 28)?

# CARING TIME                                    15 Min.
## APPLY THE LESSON AND PRAY FOR ONE ANOTHER

**LEADER**

Encourage everyone to participate in this important time and be sure that each group member is receiving prayer support. Continue to pray for the empty chair in the closing group prayer.

Following the example of Paul in verse 23, take some time now to strengthen and help one another in prayer.

1.  What season are you experiencing in your spiritual life right now?
    ❒ The warmth of summer
    ❒ The new life of spring
    ❒ The dead of winter
    ❒ The changes of fall

2.  What have been some new understandings you have gleaned from this study of Acts? What in your own life has this study particularly challenged?

3.  How could you encourage and strengthen a brother or sister in Christ in the coming week?

### NEXT WEEK

Today we were reminded how even the most learned and charismatic person, like Apollos, can sometimes use guidance and mentoring. In the coming week, write a note of thanks to your pastor or someone who has helped you on your spiritual walk. Next week we will consider the reaction of the people of Ephesus when they perceive Christianity as being a threat to their way of life. We will see God intervene as the people riot and turn against the Christians.

# NOTES ON ACTS 18:18–28

**Summary:** What the church was bringing about in the book of Acts may be described as nothing less than a quiet revolution. Perhaps the most visible aspect of that revolution was the role of women in Jewish society. Previous to Jesus, women were not allowed to study Scripture and were not supposed to follow a rabbi. Whatever spiritual knowledge they attained was to be gleaned from their husbands or the other men in their life. But women became an important part of Jesus' following (see, for example, Luke 8:1–3). In Acts, this goes a step further as women start to take teaching and leadership roles. In this story, the name of Priscilla is listed ahead of her husband Aquila. That is virtually unprecedented and indicates that she was considered the most influential of the two. That she evidently takes a prominent role in teaching proper theology to a learned man like Apollos was a major step forward in this Christian revolution. Romans 16:3–4 tells us that she and her husband risked their lives for Paul. Women like Lydia (16:11–15,40), Chloe (1 Cor. 1:11), and Phoebe (Rom. 16:1–2) were also influential in this revolution.

Another way in which Christianity took a major step forward in this passage relates to Apollos. For the most part, Christianity took root and grew among the uneducated poor and working people—fishermen, those with disabilities, lepers and prostitutes. But with Apollos, the faith got a foothold among the intelligentsia of the era. He was from Alexandria, a major intellectual and cultural center of the day. In fact, Ptolemy of Greece wanted Alexandria to be the intellectual capital of the world. Tradition says that John Mark brought Christianity to Alexandria, and that he was martyred in A.D. 62 for protesting against the worship of Serapis in that city. Later, Alexandria became a Christian intellectual center with such "Church Fathers" as Clement of Alexandria and Origen teaching in the city. All of this is to say that Apollos may have been an important link to the spreading of the Gospel to the most educated people of the day.

Our passage says that Apollos went to Achaia, another name for Greece. Corinth was a city where he apparently had a great deal of influence.

**18:18** *accompanied by Priscilla and Aquila.* It is significant that Priscilla's name is listed first, ahead of her husband. This was hardly ever done, and probably indicates that Priscilla was the more influential leader of the two. *he had his hair cut off ... because of a vow.* Pious Jews would take vows, based on the pattern of the Nazirites (Num. 6:1–21), as an indication of their devotion to God. Since the cutting of one's hair indicated the termination of the vow, Paul may have made a vow of dedication to God for as long as he was in Corinth, in gratefulness to God's promise of protection (v. 10). While normally vows would be terminated by shav-

ing one's head and offering a sacrifice in the temple at Jerusalem, people far from the city could shave their heads where they were and carry the trimmings to the temple to be presented along with a sacrifice at that time. Luke may have included this incident as evidence that Paul did not abandon the traditions of his people. *Cenchrea.* A port city near Corinth (Rom. 16:1).

**18:19–21** The positive response to Paul among the Jews at Ephesus sets the stage for his return to that city in Acts 19:1. Priscilla and Aquila stayed on at Ephesus and established the new church there.

**18:22–23** Because of his vow, Paul undoubtedly went to Jerusalem to offer a thank offering. Then he proceeded to Antioch, the church that had spawned his missionary work in the first place (13:1–3). He may have stayed there until the spring (A.D. 52 or 53), when traveling would again be possible. From there he visited the cities throughout the area where he had established churches on his first trip (13:13–14:20).

**18:23 *strengthening all the disciples.*** Paul was not the kind of evangelist who was only interested in saving souls in order to "put notches on his spiritual belt." He was also very careful to come back to them to nurture them along the way (see also Acts 14:21–22).

**18:24–28** During Paul's journey, Apollos visited Ephesus. While Apollos is a minor figure in Acts (nothing more is said of him after 19:1), he was a significant figure in the church at Corinth and became a valued associate of Paul's (1 Cor. 1:12; 3:4–23; 4:6; 16:12; perhaps 2 Cor. 8:22). Some modern scholars, following Luther, wonder if he might have authored Hebrews. This incident, as well as that in 19:1–7, shows that Acts records only a small part of the story of how the Gospel was spread throughout the known world. While unfortunately their stories are not recorded, the other apostles, as well as many unknown believers, played important roles in spreading the story of Jesus far beyond Judea.

**18:24 *Alexandria.*** A major cultural center on the northern coast of Egypt. Jews from this area were present at Pentecost and undoubtedly carried the message back home (2:10).

**18:25** While Apollos was an earnest, articulate believer in Jesus, he had not received the whole story of the Gospel. Just what he was lacking is unclear, but, as the story in 19:1–7 indicates, he may not have heard of the coming of the Spirit promised to those who are baptized in the name of Jesus.

**18:26 *Priscilla and Aquila.*** Once again Priscilla's name is mentioned first, indicating her primacy. Here it is especially significant because she is taking it on herself to instruct an educated man. That her husband was with her probably made this more socially acceptable, but it appears she was an active part of the instruction, a radical step for the time. ***the way of God.*** The various sermons in Acts record what Luke considered essential for the understanding of "the way."

**18:27–28** Whether the church at Ephesus encouraged Apollos to go to Corinth or if they encouraged the Corinthians to receive Apollos is uncertain from the Greek, and either is possible. Because of Apollos' zeal, scriptural understanding, classical education and ability to communicate, they may have felt he would be perfect for the sophisticated, worldly atmosphere at Corinth. At a later date Paul likewise encouraged Apollos to return to Corinth, but he refused to do so (1 Cor. 16:12), perhaps because he wanted nothing to do with the faction in the Corinthian church that favored him over Paul.

**18:27 *he was a great help to those who by grace had believed.*** Literally, "he contributed much to the ones having believed through grace." Two readings are possible. The NIV lays the emphasis on God's grace to the Corinthians, which caused them to believe. It can also be translated as "he contributed much through grace to the believers," putting the emphasis on Apollos' ability as a gift from God useful for helping the believers.

# A Riot in Ephesus

SCRIPTURE  ACTS 19:23–41

**LAST WEEK—**

Last week we discussed the importance of mentoring in the early church, and saw the example of Apollos being mentored by Priscilla and Aquila. We also saw Paul traveling about and "strengthening all the disciples" (Acts 18:23), reminding us that we all need to support and encourage one another. Today's session will focus on a controversy that heats up in Ephesus as the news of Christianity spreads.

## ICE-BREAKER                                           15 Min.
### CONNECT WITH YOUR GROUP

**LEADER**

Choose one or two of the Ice-Breaker questions. If you have a new group member you may want to do all three. Remember to stick closely to the three-part agenda and the time allowed for each segment.

News reports remind us that the world is filled with crisis situations. On top of that, we have to deal with many personal challenges that can come along. Take turns sharing some of your unique life experiences with moments of crisis.

1. When you were in grade school, what was the biggest crisis you faced at school?

2. What has been the closest you have come to being in a riot?
   ❐ An actual street riot.
   ❐ A riotous crowd at a game or concert.
   ❐ A sale at your favorite department store.
   ❐ Other _____.

3. In the moments of crisis in your life, who has supplied the voice of reason?

# BIBLE STUDY

## READ SCRIPTURE AND DISCUSS

# 30 Min.

**LEADER**

Select a member of the group ahead of time to real aloud the passage. Then discuss the Questions for Interaction, dividing into subgroups of four or five.

When the Gospel is shared, you can be sure that opposition will follow. The truth is often hard to accept and can be very threatening. In today's passage, the craftsmen of Ephesus feel their very livelihood is going to be destroyed if they don't put a quick stop to this new religion called "the Way." Read Acts 19:23–41 and note how the situation is resolved.

## A Riot in Ephesus

[23]*About that time there arose a great disturbance about the Way.* [24]*A silversmith named Demetrius, who made silver shrines of Artemis, brought in no little business for the craftsmen.* [25]*He called them together, along with the workmen in related trades, and said: "Men, you know we receive a good income from this business.* [26]*And you see and hear how this fellow Paul has convinced and led astray large numbers of people here in Ephesus and in practically the whole province of Asia. He says that man-made gods are no gods at all.* [27]*There is danger not only that our trade will lose its good name, but also that the temple of the great goddess Artemis will be discredited, and the goddess herself, who is worshiped throughout the province of Asia and the world, will be robbed of her divine majesty."*

[28]*When they heard this, they were furious and began shouting: "Great is Artemis of the Ephesians!"* [29]*Soon the whole city was in an uproar. The people seized Gaius and Aristarchus, Paul's traveling companions from Macedonia, and rushed as one man into the theater.* [30]*Paul wanted to appear before the crowd, but the disciples would not let him.* [31]*Even some of the officials of the province, friends of Paul, sent him a message begging him not to venture into the theater.*

[32]*The assembly was in confusion: Some were shouting one thing, some another. Most of the people did not even know why they were there.* [33]*The Jews pushed Alexander to the front, and some of the crowd shouted instructions to him. He motioned for silence in order to make a defense before the people.* [34]*But when they realized he was a Jew, they all shouted in unison for about two hours: "Great is Artemis of the Ephesians!"*

[35]*The city clerk quieted the crowd and said: "Men of Ephesus, doesn't all the world know that the city of Ephesus is the guardian of the temple of the great Artemis and of her image, which fell from heaven?* [36]*Therefore, since these facts are undeniable, you ought to be quiet and not do anything rash.* [37]*You have brought these men here, though they have neither robbed temples nor blasphemed our goddess.* [38]*If, then, Demetrius and his fellow craftsmen have a grievance against anybody, the courts are open and*

*there are proconsuls. They can press charges. [39]If there is anything further you want to bring up, it must be settled in a legal assembly. [40]As it is, we are in danger of being charged with rioting because of today's events. In that case we would not be able to account for this commotion, since there is no reason for it." [41]After he had said this, he dismissed the assembly.*

*Acts 19:23–41*

## QUESTIONS FOR INTERACTION

**LEADER**

Refer to the Summary and Study Notes at the end of this session as needed. If 30 minutes is not enough time to answer all of the questions in this section, conclude the Bible Study by answering question #7.

**1.** With whom do you identify the most in this story, and why?

**2.** When have you been in a place where, like some in this crowd, you didn't even know why you were there?

**3.** What did the craftsmen of Ephesus do to avoid listening to any voice of reason?

**4.** Had you been called upon to moderate the dispute between Paul and the "local silversmith's union," what might you have said?

**5.** If you were to put a percentage on the degree Demetrius was concerned with his income, and the degree he was concerned about Artemis being robbed of her "divine majesty," what percentage would you assign to both?

**6.** What should a Christian businessperson do when faced with a questionable business practice that is contrary to God's Word but helps to improve profits?

**7.** Complete this sentence: "A time that I, like Demetrius in this story, resisted a spiritual truth because it threatened my established way of life was when ..."

**GOING DEEPER:** *If your group has time and/or wants a challenge, go on to this question.*

**8.** What role should the church take in relationship to the business world in our country?
  ❏ A prophetic body that challenges the validity of businesses involved in questionable trades (like with the crafting of silver goddesses in Ephesus).
  ❏ A patriotic body that supports business as good for America.
  ❏ A little of both or something in between.

# CARING TIME                                     15 Min.
## APPLY THE LESSON AND PRAY FOR ONE ANOTHER

**LEADER**

Be sure to save at least 15 minutes for this time of prayer and encouragement. Continue to encourage group members to invite new people to the group.

As the disciples were concerned about Paul's welfare in today's reading (v. 30), come together now and show your concern for one another in this time of sharing and prayer.

**1.** How is your relationship with Jesus Christ right now?
   ❐ Close
   ❐ Distant
   ❐ Strained
   ❐ Other _____.

**2.** When have you been silent about your faith because you were afraid of being ridiculed? When have you boldly shared your faith? What happened as a result?

**3.** What world crisis disturbs you the most right now? What personal crisis would you like the group to pray about?

### NEXT WEEK

Today we considered some of the strong opposition that the early Christians faced. As God protected Paul in his moment of crisis in today's Scripture passage, so he will protect us and remain faithful. In the coming week, pray daily for the strength to follow God's Word in spite of opposition and pressure to do otherwise. Next week we will be encouraged by Paul's farewell address to the Ephesian elders, as he reminds the elders and us of the gift of God's grace.

# NOTES ON ACTS 19:23–41

**Summary:** Sometimes the truth of the Gospel means challenging whatever culture we are seeking to speak to. One of the aspects of our culture we especially need to challenge is our money-first orientation. Unfortunately, however, a money-first orientation is not peculiar to our time and culture, as we see in our Scripture passage.

Paul had one of his most successful mission ventures at Ephesus. He worked there for approximately three years. What had become a typical pattern for Paul—the Jewish religious leadership driving him out of town for challenging their traditions—never happened here. Instead, opposition eventually came from a far more mundane direction. A silversmith named Demetrius aroused his fellow craftsmen into a frenzy because Paul was getting people to turn away from their handcrafted goddesses. Essentially the people of Ephesus were saying, "It's all right to teach whatever you want—just don't let it interfere with business!" In this city the silver trade had become big because there were gods and goddesses to be made. The silversmith trade especially made a great deal of money through the manufacture and sale of models of the goddess Artemis. Artemis was a goddess who combined belief in the Roman virgin goddess Diana with an Asian fertility goddess. The center for her worship was in Ephesus where an image of her (actually a meteorite) was placed in a temple that was one of the seven wonders of the ancient world. In the spring, there was a festival in her honor marked by crowds flocking to Ephesus for a celebration that included orgies and general carousing. Teaching that there was one God, who was not made with human hands, and that God demanded right living and sexual responsibility really interfered with this business-building festival!

Once Demetrius had convinced the craftsmen that their livelihood was at stake, they stopped listening to anyone else. They repeatedly yelled out, "Great is Artemis of the Ephesians!" Alexander was almost able to quiet them down to listen, until they realized that he was a Jew. The people of Ephesus didn't make any distinction between Jews and Christians at this time. As far as they were concerned, they were all part of that Jewish faith that insisted on worshiping one God, and didn't tolerate gods made by their hands. So then we are told they went on shouting. "Great is Artemis of the Ephesians" for two more hours!

The Ephesian silversmiths shut their ears to everything in their desperate clinging to "business as usual." But they were clinging to an empty way of life. The days of their craft were numbered, and they were living under the illusion that something they made with their own hands could be a god. This story is a warning to us against making the same mistake.

**19:29 *Gaius and Aristarchus.*** These men were among those who accompanied Paul when he left Ephesus (20:4). Unable to find Paul, the crowd grabbed two of his associates to accuse. **the theater.** While this was the usual place for public meetings, it would have been especially appropriate in this case since the great temple of Artemis could be clearly seen from it!

**19:30–31** Both the Christians and some of the officials (these were the *asiarchs*, the chief citizens out of whose ranks the officials of the Roman cult of emperor worship were elected for one-year terms of office) urged Paul not to go into the theater for fear of his safety. The protection of the *asiarchs* is another example of official Roman protection and tolerance of Paul (18:14–17).

**19:33–34** The Jews, perhaps to disassociate themselves from the charges being made against Paul, tried to have one of their number (Alexander) make a statement. However, since the Jews were well known to be against idolatry as well, the crowd shouted him down before he could even speak.

**19:35** *city clerk.* This was the highest-ranking official in the city accountable to the Roman provincial government for what happened in Ephesus. Not wanting to be charged with rioting, which could lead to penalties for the city, he worked to quiet down the crowd and dismiss them.

**19:37** *robbed temples.* Wealthy people would deposit treasures at temples for safekeeping in light of the sacred nature of the place.

**19:38** *proconsuls.* The Roman Senate through a proconsul administered provinces that did not require troops to maintain order. Typically, there was only one at a time over a given area.

**19:39** *legal assembly.* The people could gather for meetings to discuss issues that concerned them, but they were to be held at set times and with a set procedure. Such an irregular, chaotic meeting as this one could lead to Roman suppression of their right to assemble. The crowd, mindful of the implied warning, dispersed.

# PAUL'S GOOD-BYE TO THE EPHESIANS

SCRIPTURE   ACTS 20:16–38

**LAST WEEK**

In last week's session we learned about the riot at Ephesus and considered how Christians continually face opposition to their faith. This opposition can take many forms, but can be overcome through faithful commitment to God. Today's lesson will focus on Paul's farewell to the Ephesian elders, where he reminds them that it is more blessed to give than to receive.

## ICE-BREAKER                    15 Min.
### CONNECT WITH YOUR GROUP

**LEADER**

Introduce and welcome new group members. If there are no new members, choose one or two of the Ice-Breaker questions to get started. If there are new members, then discuss all three.

Life consists of many happy hellos and difficult good-byes. Take turns sharing your experiences with saying good-bye and planning your journey along the road of life.

1.  What is the hardest good-bye you have ever had to say? What made that good-bye so difficult?

2.  What is your "itinerary" for this coming week's "journey"? What "stops" do you look forward to? Which ones do you wish you could avoid?

3.  If you knew you would have to leave your friends tomorrow and never see them again, what parting advice would you want to give them?

# BIBLE STUDY
## READ SCRIPTURE AND DISCUSS

## 30 Min.

**LEADER**

Have two members of the group, selected ahead of time, read aloud the passage. Ask one member to read the part of Luke, the narrator, and the other to read the part of Paul. Then discuss the Questions for Interaction, dividing into subgroups of four or five.

Paul made many friends during his travels and deeply loved his brothers and sisters in Christ. In today's Scripture passage, he passes along a final word of hope and encouragement as he says good-bye to the Ephesian elders. Read Acts 20:16–38 and note the important points Paul makes about God's grace and the importance of giving, rather than receiving.

## Paul's Farewell to the Ephesian Elders

Luke: *<sup>16</sup>Paul had decided to sail past Ephesus to avoid spending time in the province of Asia, for he was in a hurry to reach Jerusalem, if possible, by the day of Pentecost. <sup>17</sup>From Miletus, Paul sent to Ephesus for the elders of the church. <sup>18</sup>When they arrived, he said to them:*

Paul: *"You know how I lived the whole time I was with you, from the first day I came into the province of Asia. <sup>19</sup>I served the Lord with great humility and with tears, although I was severely tested by the plots of the Jews. <sup>20</sup>You know that I have not hesitated to preach anything that would be helpful to you but have taught you publicly and from house to house. <sup>21</sup>I have declared to both Jews and Greeks that they must turn to God in repentance and have faith in our Lord Jesus.*

*<sup>22</sup>"And now, compelled by the Spirit, I am going to Jerusalem, not knowing what will happen to me there. <sup>23</sup>I only know that in every city the Holy Spirit warns me that prison and hardships are facing me. <sup>24</sup>However, I consider my life worth nothing to me, if only I may finish the race and complete the task the Lord Jesus has given me—the task of testifying to the gospel of God's grace.*

*<sup>25</sup>"Now I know that none of you among whom I have gone about preaching the kingdom will ever see me again. <sup>26</sup>Therefore, I declare to you today that I am innocent of the blood of all men. <sup>27</sup>For I have not hesitated to proclaim to you the whole will of God. <sup>28</sup>Keep watch over yourselves and all the flock of which the Holy Spirit has made you overseers. Be shepherds of the church of God, which he bought with his own blood. <sup>29</sup>I know that after I leave, savage wolves will come in among you and will not spare the flock. <sup>30</sup>Even from your own number men will arise and distort the truth in order to draw away disciples after them. <sup>31</sup>So be on your guard! Remember that for three years I never stopped warning each of you night and day with tears.*

*<sup>32</sup>"Now I commit you to God and to the word of his grace, which can build you up and give you an inheritance among all those who are sanctified. <sup>33</sup>I have not coveted anyone's silver or gold or clothing. <sup>34</sup>You yourselves know that these hands of mine have supplied my own needs and the needs of my companions. <sup>35</sup>In everything I did, I showed you that by this kind of hard work*

*we must help the weak, remembering the words the Lord Jesus himself said:*
*'It is more blessed to give than to receive.' "*

Luke: *³⁶When he had said this, he knelt down with all of them and prayed. ³⁷They all wept as they embraced him and kissed him. ³⁸What grieved them most was his statement that they would never see his face again. Then they accompanied him to the ship.*

*Acts 20:16–38*

**LEADER**

Refer to the Summary and Study Notes at the conclusion of this session. If 30 minutes is not enough time to answer all of the questions in this section, conclude the Bible Study by answering question #7.

## QUESTIONS FOR INTERACTION

1. Had you been one of Paul's Ephesian friends, how would you have reacted to his words?
   ❏ Insisted that he not go?
   ❏ Insisted that you go with him.
   ❏ Just cried and said good-bye.
   ❏ Just ignored his words of gloom and believed the best.
   ❏ Other _____.

2. Why does Paul feel the need to remind the Ephesian elders how he had lived "the whole time he was with them"?
   ❏ To make them feel obligated to him.
   ❏ To urge them to follow his example and carry on his work.
   ❏ Just to reminisce with them.
   ❏ Other _____.

3. What is Paul's central goal at this point of his life? Where must he go as part of fulfilling this goal?

4. What does Paul predict will happen after he leaves? What does he call on the Ephesian elders to do in response to this warning?

5. In what ways did Paul exemplify Jesus' teaching quoted here, "It is more blessed to give than to receive"?

6. What have you experienced that has helped you better understand how blessed it is to be able to give to others?

7. How well are you balancing what you are giving in life with what you have received? In what specific areas might God be calling you to give more?

**GOING DEEPER:** *If your group has time and/or wants a challenge, go on to this question.*

**8.** How should a Christian relate to a friend or loved one who decides to take on a dangerous task or mission because he or she feels God is calling them to it? How do you know when the person is just being a foolhardy martyr, and when he or she is following in the footsteps of Paul?

# CARING TIME         15 Min.

### APPLY THE LESSON AND PRAY FOR ONE ANOTHER

**LEADER**

Continue to encourage group members to invite new people to the group. Remind everyone that this group is for learning and sharing, but also for reaching out to others. Close the group prayer by thanking God for each member and for this time together.

Encourage and support one another in this Caring Time. Take turns sharing your responses to the following questions. Then share prayer requests and close with prayer.

**1.** What was the high point of last week for you? What was the low point?

**2.** How has God's grace been a gift to you? To whom would you like to pass this gift along?

**3.** What "savage wolves" (v. 29) will you be facing this coming week that will try to keep you from focusing on God's plan for your life?

---

### NEXT WEEK

Today we listened in on a beautiful good-bye that Paul said to the Ephesian elders. He encouraged them and reminded them of Jesus' words: "It is more blessed to give than to receive." In the coming week, give the gift of your time to a family member, friend or neighbor who is lonely or needs encouragement. Next week we will continue to follow Paul's ministry as he arrives in Jerusalem. Paul encounters a great trial there when he is attacked by an angry mob and arrested by Roman troops.

# NOTES ON ACTS 20:16–38

**Summary:** Great leaders lead not just in their lifetime—they give guidance that stays with their followers as those followers carry on their work. Jesus took the time after his resurrection to "open the minds" of his disciples so they could understand the Scriptures (Luke 24:45). He wanted them to constantly turn to God's Word as a guide to help them in the work they would do after he left. Martin Luther King, Jr. urged his followers to hang on to their hope for a better world, even though as he said in one of his latter speeches, "I may not get there with you." In this passage from the twentieth chapter of Acts, Paul also, as a great leader, is preparing his followers for what they needed to do after he was gone. He warns them "none of you among whom I have gone about preaching the kingdom will ever see me again" (v. 25). Because he would never see them again, he does two things: (1) he reminds them of how he had worked among them, not as a way of bragging, but as a way of pointing out the example he had set for them to follow (vv. 26–27 and vv. 34–35); and (2) he makes a specific list of things they need to do to make sure their church would continue to thrive. These needed actions included keeping watch over their "flock" (v. 28), being on their guard for those who might lead the people astray (vv. 28–29), and committing themselves to God's Word (v. 32).

Paul's good-bye to his friends in Ephesus was a sad event. But it would have been a much sadder event if he had not prepared them to thrive after he was gone. Then the church that Paul had started would have ended. Indeed, Paul had earlier worried this might happen when he had to prematurely leave a young church in Thessalonica, but, perhaps in part because of the work of Timothy, this was not the case (1 Thess. 2:17–3:13). In Ephesus, the work of Christ started by Paul also thrived for some time afterward. Revelation later lauded the Ephesian church for the way they resisted false teaching (Rev. 2:1–3), and the apostle John probably spent the last years of his ministry in this vital church.

**20:16** Luke traces Paul's four-day journey of about 100 miles from Troas to Miletus, where he addressed the elders of the Ephesian church.

**20:19** In the Greek world, humility was seen as a weakness—a sign of a slave. For Paul, however, who saw himself as a slave for God (Rom. 1:1), humility was essential for discipleship (Phil. 2:3; Col. 3:12).

**20:20** Paul's ministry was the same whether in full view of the public (as in the school of Tyrannus—19:9) or in the confines of a small house church (the normal meeting place for groups of believers).

**20:21** *repentance/faith.* While Paul might stress to Gentiles their need to turn from idols to God (17:29–30; 1 Thess. 1:9) and to Jews their need to have faith in God rather than in their own works for justification (13:39), repentance and faith are two sides of the same coin in terms of how one is to respond to God.

**20:23** *in every city the Holy Spirit warns me that prison and hardships are facing me.* Paul was undertaking this journey in full conviction that God wanted him to go, but also with an awareness that it would lead to difficulty. All along the way, the Spirit was preparing him for the hardships he would face at his destination. This sense of foreboding led him to ask the Roman church to pray for him as he went (Rom. 15:30–32).

**20:24** *finish the race.* Just prior to his death, Paul wrote to Timothy at Ephesus using this same metaphor to describe his ministry (2 Tim. 4:7). *the gospel of God's grace.* Just as repentance and faith sum up what it means to respond to God, so grace sums up the news of what God has done for us (Rom. 5:1–11; Eph. 2:8–9).

**20:25** *none of you ... will ever see me again.* A few weeks earlier, Paul wrote to the Romans that after he went to Jerusalem he hoped to visit them and proceed to Spain since his work in Macedonia and Achaia (and presumably Asia) was accomplished (Rom. 15:23). Whether this is why he says he will not see these people again or whether he subsequently felt that the warnings of the Spirit (v. 23) are to prepare him for death is uncertain.

**20:26–27** Using the imagery from Ezekiel 33:1–6, Paul asserts he has been like a faithful watchman and "is innocent of the blood of all men." He therefore can't be faulted for any problems that may arise in the church.

**20:28** *the flock.* The Old Testament often used this image for Israel (Ps. 100:3; Isa. 40:11). *overseers.* This word is translated elsewhere as "bishops." Elders, bishops and pastors are synonymous terms in the New Testament. They imply the responsibility of caring for the spiritual needs of others. *his own blood.* Since nowhere else in the New Testament is it said that God shed his blood, the phrase most likely refers to Jesus who is called God's "own son" in Romans 8:32.

**20:29–31** The call to be on the watch is necessary because, as Paul has learned through hard experience, there will come times of opposition both from without and from within. At this time, the external opposition was primarily from Jews (v. 19) while internal opposition arose through false teachers who claimed the Gospel Paul preached was insufficient (2 Cor. 11:4–6).

**20:33** *silver or gold or clothing.* Common symbols of wealth. The fact that Paul worked for a living while in Ephesus was proof that he never used his position to try to get anything from the people.

**20:35** *the words the Lord Jesus himself said* ... This beatitude is not found in the Gospels. It is similar to a Greek proverb, which Jesus may have adapted for his own use. Paul only quotes Jesus twice elsewhere (1 Cor. 7:10; 1 Tim. 5:18).

# Session 8
# Paul Arrested

Scripture   Acts 21:17–36

## LAST WEEK

We were inspired last week by the beautiful good-bye that Paul said to the Ephesian elders. He not only said good-bye, but also reminded them and us of many truths that will keep us on the right path and help us stay true to the Christian faith. This week we will begin to see the importance of that good-bye. Paul is arrested in Jerusalem and begins going through a long legal process to try to attain his freedom.

## ICE-BREAKER                                    15 Min.
### Connect with your Group

**LEADER**

Choose one, two or all three of the Ice-Breaker questions. Be sure to welcome and introduce new group members.

Paul faced many situations that were full of embarrassment and conflict. Take turns sharing your own experiences with trying circumstances.

**1.** What was the most embarrassing haircut you have ever gotten? Ever get a "buzz cut"?

**2.** When do you remember getting people so angry with you that they could have killed you?
❑ When you disobeyed your parents as a teenager.
❑ When you messed up at work.
❑ When you embarrassed your spouse.
❑ Other _____.

**3.** When do you remember being the victim of a big misunderstanding? How did it happen and did you ever get things cleared up?

# BIBLE STUDY

### READ SCRIPTURE AND DISCUSS

# 30 Min.

**LEADER**

Select a member of the group ahead of time to read aloud the Scripture passage. Then discuss the Questions for Interaction, dividing into subgroups of four or five.

Paul had had so many triumphs in sharing Christ and starting churches that you would think he would have been treated with great honor when he returned to the mother church in Jerusalem. However, while some greeted him warmly, others turned on him. Read Acts 21:17–36 and see what it says to us about facing such conflicts.

## Paul Arrested

¹⁷*When we arrived at Jerusalem, the brothers received us warmly.* ¹⁸*The next day Paul and the rest of us went to see James, and all the elders were present.* ¹⁹*Paul greeted them and reported in detail what God had done among the Gentiles through his ministry.*

²⁰*When they heard this, they praised God. Then they said to Paul: "You see, brother, how many thousands of Jews have believed, and all of them are zealous for the law.* ²¹*They have been informed that you teach all the Jews who live among the Gentiles to turn away from Moses, telling them not to circumcise their children or live according to our customs.* ²²*What shall we do? They will certainly hear that you have come,* ²³*so do what we tell you. There are four men with us who have made a vow.* ²⁴*Take these men, join in their purification rites and pay their expenses, so that they can have their heads shaved. Then everybody will know there is no truth in these reports about you, but that you yourself are living in obedience to the law.* ²⁵*As for the Gentile believers, we have written to them our decision that they should abstain from food sacrificed to idols, from blood, from the meat of strangled animals and from sexual immorality."*

²⁶*The next day Paul took the men and purified himself along with them. Then he went to the temple to give notice of the date when the days of purification would end and the offering would be made for each of them.*

²⁷*When the seven days were nearly over, some Jews from the province of Asia saw Paul at the temple. They stirred up the whole crowd and seized him,* ²⁸*shouting, "Men of Israel, help us! This is the man who teaches all men everywhere against our people and our law and this place. And besides, he has brought Greeks into the temple area and defiled this holy place."*

²⁹*(They had previously seen Trophimus the Ephesian in the city with Paul and assumed that Paul had brought him into the temple area.)*

³⁰*The whole city was aroused, and the people came running*

*from all directions. Seizing Paul, they dragged him from the temple, and immediately the gates were shut. ³¹While they were trying to kill him, news reached the commander of the Roman troops that the whole city of Jerusalem was in an uproar. ³²He at once took some officers and soldiers and ran down to the crowd. When the rioters saw the commander and his soldiers, they stopped beating Paul.*

*    ³³The commander came up and arrested him and ordered him to be bound with two chains. Then he asked who he was and what he had done. ³⁴Some in the crowd shouted one thing and some another, and since the commander could not get at the truth because of the uproar, he ordered that Paul be taken into the barracks. ³⁵When Paul reached the steps, the violence of the mob was so great he had to be carried by the soldiers. ³⁶The crowd that followed kept shouting, "Away with him!"*

*Acts 21:17–36*

## LEADER

Refer to the Summary and Study Notes at the end of this session as needed. If 30 minutes is not enough time to answer all of the questions in this section, conclude the Bible study by answering question #7.

## QUESTIONS FOR INTERACTION

**1.** Had you been Paul, how would you have felt about James' proposal to be part of the vow these men were making?

❑ Eager to cooperate and please.

❑ Irritated at having to "jump through hoops."

❑ Like a phony, compromising politician.

❑ Other _____.

**2.** Why does James refer here (v. 25) to the decision of the Jerusalem Council (see 15:20)?

❑ To let Paul know that they had compromised and so should he.

❑ To let Paul know they were still planning to abide by that agreement.

❑ Other _____.

**3.** Who do the Jews from Asia think Paul has taken into the temple area? Why do they think this? What might they have done to check this out had they been acting more rationally?

**4.** What saves Paul from being beaten to death at this point? What is the interest of the commander of the Roman troops? Does he respond as a responsible law-enforcement official?

**5.** Why was the crowd so quick to judge Paul as guilty?

❑ They had heard and believed rumors.

❑ They were over-defensive of their faith because of the hostile environment.

❑ They were just angry and out for a scapegoat.

❑ Other _____.

**6.** Under what circumstances have you seen people being quick to judge? What causes people to behave in such a way?

**7.** For what strong conviction would you risk getting arrested?

**GOING DEEPER:** *If your group has time and/or wants a challenge, go on to this question.*

**8.** When is it important to conform to what someone else believes to be important, and when should a person simply "be true to themselves"? What do you learn from Paul's experience in this regard?

# CARING TIME 15 Min.
## APPLY THE LESSONS AND PRAY FOR ONE ANOTHER

**LEADER**

Have you started working with your group about their mission—perhaps by sharing the dream of multiplying into two groups by the end of this study of Acts?

God remained faithful to Paul through many difficult and trying times. Let us now take our trials and difficulties to God, encouraging and supporting each other with a time of sharing and prayer.

**1.** Share with the group a spiritual struggle or victory from this last week.

**2.** What need or emotional stress has had you "locked up or imprisoned" lately? Would you rate your experience as being in "maximum security," "minimum security," "house arrest" or "work release"?

**3.** Who is giving you a hard time right now, like these people gave to Paul? How would you like us to pray for this person or persons?

Today we saw the dramatic and violent results of the misunderstanding and hatred that many of the Jews in Jerusalem had toward Paul and what he was teaching. We may not experience resistance to this degree, but in many ways our society is just as intolerant of Christianity. In the coming week, pray for boldness to speak up for Jesus when he is made fun of or ridiculed. Next week we will learn about the legal process that Paul has to go through to obtain his freedom, and we will see how he reacts when on trial for his life and faith. This study will give us an opportunity to think about how we would react under similar circumstances.

# NOTES ON ACTS 21:17–36

**Summary:** It's been said, "There's simply no pleasing some people," and that was certainly Paul's experience in this story. He did all that he could be expected to do in order to heal the rift between himself and those Jews who were zealous for Jewish ceremonial law. He had earlier been part of the meeting in Jerusalem where it was determined that Gentiles need not be circumcised (ch. 15). He had worked hard to collect an offering for those in need in Jerusalem, an offering that he doubtlessly delivered on this trip. And upon arriving in Jerusalem he agreed to participate in the religious vows of four Jewish Christians by paying the expenses related to their purification rites. What more could he have done? Unfortunately, it seems that there were some who had already made up their minds that Paul presented a threat to their faith and tradition. These people decided to take advantage of the fact that many of those who were zealous for the law were present in Jerusalem. This was their best chance to bring down this man who taught that people could find righteousness with God without the ceremonial law.

The events of this chapter show that there was obviously a lot of pent-up anger in Jerusalem. Not all of it related to Paul, although he became the focus of it. People were angry at the foreign domination of Rome. People were probably angry at the economic conditions that made the offering that Paul and his associates brought necessary. And some who had not believed in Christ were angry that this new teaching had captured the imagination and passion of the people more than the Jewish ceremonial traditions. All of this taken together resulted in an anger that overflowed without restraint—"When Paul reached the steps, the violence of the mob was so great he had to be carried by the soldiers. The crowd that followed kept shouting, 'Away with him!' " (vv. 35–36).

As was the case with Jesus, Paul's arrest was an injustice. He would stay under arrest for years, and many believe he was never free again before his execution. That such unjust events happen in this world in which we live may depress some of us. But the fact that it happened to Jesus, the very Son of God, and to Paul, his greatest missionary, should remind us we are not alone when it happens to us. It should also remind us that it is through such events that God is establishing his kingdom "on earth as it is in heaven," a kingdom where justice will prevail. Christ's death after an unjust trial brought us forgiveness. Paul's death inspired his followers to carry on his work, as the church spread like wildfire throughout Europe and Asia. And the deaths of Christian martyrs throughout the ages have only further fueled that fire.

**21:17-19** It was undoubtedly at this meeting with James (Jesus' half-brother and the spokesperson for the church in Jerusalem) that Paul and his companions presented the offering from the Gentile churches. This meeting also allowed Paul an opportunity to update James and the others on all that had happened since his last visit to Jerusalem.

**21:20-21** If Jewish believers in Rome could still be rigid about the dietary and Sabbath laws (Rom. 14:2,5), how much more would these Judean believers, having lived all their lives in a strictly Jewish environment, be opposed to any hint that their customs were being ignored? Paul's letters reveal that even after the council's decision in chapter 15 he was consistently troubled by Palestinian believers who insisted his Gospel was deficient in that he did not require the observance of Jewish laws (Phil. 3:2-3; Col. 2:16).

**21:22-24** To prove that Paul still honored the Jewish customs, it was suggested that he personally and financially participate in a vow that four of the elders themselves had made. Although commentators are unsure what the nature of the vow was since the time frame involved does not seem to fit in with known practices, it may have been in connection with the rules for the defilement of a Nazirite vow in Numbers 6:9-12.

**21:25** To reinforce that this action applied only to Paul as a Jew, James (or Luke as the editor) repeats the decision of the council (15:22-29).

**21:26** In keeping with his policy of acting in whatever way would provide the least resistance for the Gospel of Christ, Paul agreed to the plan (1 Cor. 9:19-21).

**21:27-29** Paul apparently had difficulties with these people before (20:18-19), but now their strong nationalist and religious sentiments, heightened by the feast, were inflamed as they assumed that Paul must have brought the Gentile Trophimus into the temple. They knew Trophimus from their contacts with him at Ephesus. While Gentiles could enter the outermost court of the temple, the inner courts—where only Jews could go—were surrounded by a low wall on which were signs that read in Greek and Latin: "No foreigner may enter within the barricade which surrounds the temple and enclosure. Anyone who is caught doing so will have himself to blame for his ensuing death."

**21:30** *The whole city.* A hyperbolic phrase, although certainly all within earshot in the temple would have come running.

**21:31-32** Paul was probably dragged outside the temple and beaten. The Roman cohort was quartered on the northwest side of the temple in the Fortress of Antonia, which was connected to the Court of the Gentiles by two staircases and commanded a view of the temple area. Ever on the alert for disturbance, especially around the times of feasts, the commander and some of his soldiers (a cohort, at least on paper, consisted of 1000 soldiers—both infantry and cavalry) raced through the crowd to the center of the action.

**21:36** *Away with him!* The violence and the cries of the crowd provide another parallel with the arrest and death of Jesus (Luke 23:18).

# SESSION 9
# PAUL BEFORE THE SANHEDRIN

SCRIPTURE   ACTS 22:30—23:11

**LAST WEEK**

In last week's session we learned of Paul's violent arrest and imprisonment in Jerusalem. But we also remembered that God's will is often accomplished through such unjust events. This week we will see how Paul reacts to being tried by the Sanhedrin, which was where religious offenses were tried in the Jewish society of the day. We will also consider how Christ reassures Paul of his presence during this very difficult time.

## ICE-BREAKER                                    15 Min.
### CONNECT WITH YOUR GROUP

**LEADER**

Welcome and introduce new group members. Choose one, two or all three Ice-Breaker questions, depending on your group's needs.

Sometimes we are caught between strong opposing forces and it becomes difficult to really know what to do. Later we will see how this happened to Paul. Take turns sharing your experiences when this has happened to you.

1. When you were in grade school, what derogatory names did you call the kids you didn't like? What derogatory names were most often used against you?

2. Have you ever made a disparaging remark about a person, only to learn that he or she was someone important—the boss's nephew, your spouse's favorite uncle, for example? How did you get out of that embarrassing situation?

3. What "opposing forces" have you found yourself caught between most often in your life?
   ❏ Your parents and your in-laws.
   ❏ "Pro-life" and "Pro-choice" people.
   ❏ Republicans and Democrats.
   ❏ Other _____.

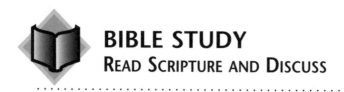

# BIBLE STUDY

## READ SCRIPTURE AND DISCUSS

# 30 Min.

**LEADER**

Select a member of the group ahead of time to read aloud the passage. Then discuss the Questions for Interaction, dividing into subgroups of four or five.

In modern society we are not put on trial for disagreeing with a religious perspective or violating a strictly religious law. But that was not true in Paul's day. So in the following story we see how he was taken before the Sanhedrin and accused of essentially "religious crimes." Read Acts 22:30–23:11 and note what Paul does well and not-so-well as he seeks to defend his actions.

## Paul Before the Sanhedrin

*30 The next day, since the commander wanted to find out exactly why Paul was being accused by the Jews, he released him and ordered the chief priests and all the Sanhedrin to assemble. Then he brought Paul and had him stand before them.*

**23** *Paul looked straight at the Sanhedrin and said, "My brothers, I have fulfilled my duty to God in all good conscience to this day." 2 At this the high priest Ananias ordered those standing near Paul to strike him on the mouth. 3 Then Paul said to him, "God will strike you, you whitewashed wall! You sit there to judge me according to the law, yet you yourself violate the law by commanding that I be struck!"*

*4 Those who were standing near Paul said, "You dare to insult God's high priest?"*

*5 Paul replied, "Brothers, I did not realize that he was the high priest; for it is written: 'Do not speak evil about the ruler of your people.' "*

*6 Then Paul, knowing that some of them were Sadducees and the others Pharisees, called out in the Sanhedrin, "My brothers, I am a Pharisee, the son of a Pharisee. I stand on trial because of my hope in the resurrection of the dead." 7 When he said this, a dispute broke out between the Pharisees and the Sadducees, and the assembly was divided. 8 (The Sadducees say that there is no resurrection, and that there are neither angels nor spirits, but the Pharisees acknowledge them all.)*

*9 There was a great uproar, and some of the teachers of the law who were Pharisees stood up and argued vigorously. "We find nothing wrong with this man," they said. "What if a spirit or an angel has spoken to him?" 10 The dispute became so violent that the commander was afraid Paul would be torn to pieces by them. He ordered the troops to go down and take him away from them by force and bring him into the barracks.*

*11 The following night the Lord stood near Paul and said, "Take courage! As you have testified about me in Jerusalem, so you must also testify in Rome."*

*Acts 22:30–23:11*

## QUESTIONS FOR INTERACTION

**LEADER**

Refer to the Summary and Study Notes at the conclusion of this session. If 30 minutes is not enough time to answer all of the questions in this section, conclude the Bible Study by answering question #7.

1. Which aspect of Paul are you more like—the temperamental Paul who verbally lashes out before he thinks? Or the politically wise Paul who devises a "divide and conquer" strategy?

2. Why do you think the High Priest has Paul struck in the face?
   - ❒ To provoke him.
   - ❒ To show who was in charge.
   - ❒ Because he thought Paul was lying.
   - ❒ Other _____.

3. Who else referred to members of the religious establishment as "whitewashed" (see Matt. 23:27)? What are some of the implications of that word?

4. Do you think Paul really didn't understand that he had spoken harshly to the High Priest, or was he just trying to cover for his rash act?

5. Over what theological issues does Paul seek to pit the Pharisees and Sadducees against each other? Is his strategy successful? Why or why not?

6. What opposing forces threaten to "tear you to pieces" right now? Who or what has saved you from this fate so far?

7. For what current task or mission do you need to "take courage"? What about that task or mission is frightening?

**GOING DEEPER:** *If your group has time and/or wants a challenge, go on to this next question.*

8. How should a Christian treat persons in authority with whom he or she strongly disagrees? Is there a time when an open expression of anger toward such people is appropriate? If so, how should such anger be expressed?

# CARING TIME                                    15 Min.

## APPLY THE LESSON AND PRAY FOR ONE ANOTHER

**LEADER**

Have you identified someone in the group that could be a leader for a new small group when your group divides? How could you encourage and mentor that person?

Our prayer time is an opportunity for taking what we have struggled with in this session, as well as in past weeks, to God for his direction and healing. Take turns sharing responses to the following questions. Then close with a time of group prayer, asking God to give you the courage to continue with the mission he has given you.

1.   What is something you did this past week to help you grow in your faith?

2.   When have you strongly felt the presence of the Lord in a difficult situation?

3.   What support or encouragement do you need from this group in regard to the task or mission you mentioned in question #7 of the Bible Study?

## NEXT WEEK

Today we considered how Paul responded to his trial before the Sanhedrin. We saw how he didn't waver in his faith, even when he knew of the consequences. In the coming week, pick two Bible verses to memorize that will help you be strong in your faith, despite pressure to do otherwise (e.g., Isa. 41:10 and Phil. 4:13). Next week we will continue to follow Paul's trial, this time before secular authorities who have the power to decide whether he will live or die. We will see how in defending himself before those authorities, Paul's faith and courage really shine forth.

# NOTES ON ACTS 22:30–23:11

**Summary:** It had almost become a tradition for Christian leaders to have a trial before the Sanhedrin where everything seems stacked against them. It happened to Christ, where the Sanhedrin had brought in false evidence (Matt. 26:59); it happened to Stephen, where false witnesses had been brought in (6:13); and now it was happening to Paul. Imagine a trial today where almost the first thing the judge does is to have the defendant struck in the face! The defense attorney would be delighted, knowing that a higher court, because of the judge's prejudicial attitude, would almost certainly overturn any negative verdict. In a sense, that was the case with Paul as well. No matter how bad this human court was treating him, he knew a "higher court"—the God of the Universe—would eventually overturn their verdict.

We also see some other realities about the Jewish religious leadership of the time. Sometimes one might get the impression that while poor people, women and Gentiles gravitated to Christianity, the traditional Jewish leadership was united in opposition to this new teaching. Here we see that such was not the case. The Sadducees opposed Paul because of his belief in the resurrection of the dead, a belief they vehemently denied (Matt. 22:23–33); and also possibly because of their connection to the temple and the sacrificial system that Paul seemed to be saying was no longer necessary because of Christ's sacrificial act. The Pharisees, while they questioned Paul's view of the law, at least agreed with him about the resurrection, as well as about the role of angelic messengers. Paul himself still considered himself a Pharisee (v. 6). He understood these differences and used them to his advantage. While the Pharisees and Sadducees got in a dispute that was so violent that some feared it would result in Paul being "torn to pieces" (v. 10), at least they were not united in their condemnation of him.

However, it was not this reality of a divided Judaism that Paul was counting on for his eventual well-being—it was the God of Jesus Christ. The only reassurance he needed was the one that comes at the end of this story, the one that comes from his Lord: "Take courage! As you have testified about me in Jerusalem, so you must also testify in Rome." He knew that the one who commissioned him to do more would also be with him in all that he was called to do.

**23:2 the high priest Ananias.** Ananias was appointed to this office by Herod Agrippa II (25:13) in A.D. 47 and held the position until A.D. 58 or 59. He had a well-established reputation for being a violent, greedy and unscrupulous man. It was suspected that he stole the offerings from the temple (there exists a parody for him based on Psalm 24 which reads, "The temple court cried out, 'Lift up your heads, O ye gates, and let (Ananias) ... and fill his stomach with divine sacrifices' ") and was involved in assassinations against those who opposed him. **ordered those standing near to Paul to strike him.** It was against Jewish law for a defendant to be treated like this. Whether Ananias did so to intimidate Paul or because he found his comments of faithful service offensive is uncertain.

**23:3 God will strike you.** Whether or not this was intended as a prophecy or simply as a comment about God's judgment against evildoers, Paul's word came true. In A.D. 66 Jews who were leading a revolt against Rome captured Ananias and murdered him for his pro-Roman policies. *you whitewashed wall!* The picture is of someone trying to fix up a wall threatening to collapse simply by painting it with a thin coat of paint. While Ananias, as a member of the Sanhedrin, had the trappings of a minister of justice, his actions betrayed that justice was far from a concern of his.

**23:4–5** Paul's response to the question of how he could speak so against the high priest is confusing, as it is unlikely he would not have known who the high priest was. Paul may be masking ignorance with irony in that his response may mean something like, "How could I be expected to know that he is the high priest given the way he acts?" He then quotes Exodus 22:28 as a half-apology for his comment and, probably, as another indication of his submission to the Law.

**23:6 *I am a Pharisee.*** See Philippians 3:4–6. Since Pharisees believed in principle in the idea of resurrection, it was easier for them to accept the resurrection of Jesus. Pharisees would at least be sympathetic with their brethren who believed in Jesus' resurrection since their overall lifestyle was consistent with Jewish piety. Paul is seeking here to utilize the division between these groups to his benefit.

**23:8 *resurrection.*** The resurrection of the dead prior to the full establishment of God's reign was a crucial doctrine for the Pharisees, but flatly rejected by the Sadducees, who, since they only accepted the five books of Moses as authoritative, found no basis for such a belief (although see Luke 20:37). It was this issue that created a division in the Sanhedrin at an earlier trial as well (5:17,33–39). ***angels/spirits.*** Since angels are spoken of in the first five books of Moses, it is probable that what the Sadducees rejected may have been a Pharisaic belief that in the resurrection people became spiritual beings like the angels and demons.

**23:9 *What if a spirit or an angel has spoken to him?*** Paul may have retold the account of his experience on the Damascus road, which some of the Pharisees may have interpreted as an appearance of Jesus' spirit.

**23:11** For the fourth and final time in Acts, the Lord addresses Paul personally to encourage him in a time of crisis (an angel comforts him in the midst of a storm in 27:23–24). ***Take courage!*** The same word is used when Jesus spoke to the disciples as they faced a life-threatening storm on the Sea of Galilee (Mark 6:50). ***testified about me.*** The real issue at stake was speaking of Jesus, not defending himself against false charges. Paul seemed to realize that in his address to the Sanhedrin (v. 6).

# PAUL BEFORE AGRIPPA AND FESTUS

SCRIPTURE   ACTS 26:19–32

## LAST WEEK

Paul's problems in Jerusalem continued in last week's Scripture reading as he stood trial before the Sanhedrin, the Jewish ruling council. We were reminded, along with Paul, that the Lord is close to us in our troubles and gives us courage. This week we will observe Paul's testimony before some of the secular authorities of Rome and consider what it means to testify to our faith in Jesus Christ in a secular world.

## ICE-BREAKER                              15 Min.
### CONNECT WITH YOUR GROUP

**LEADER**

Choose one or two of the Ice-Breaker questions. If you have a new group member you may want to do all three. Remember to stick closely to the three-part agenda and the time allowed for each segment.

Paul is told in today's story that his great learning has driven him insane. How about you? Take turns sharing what kind of learning you have and how it affects your behavior.

1. What do you consider to be the most "insane" thing you have ever done?
   ❐ Gone swimming in an icy lake in January.
   ❐ Volunteered to chaperone a teenager's party.
   ❐ Taught a teenager to drive.
   ❐ Went for an evening stroll in a high crime area.
   ❐ Other _____.

2. In what areas of study do you have the most "book learning"? In what areas do you have the most learning from experience?

3. In respect to what abilities or behaviors might you encourage others to become like you?

# BIBLE STUDY

## READ SCRIPTURE AND DISCUSS

# 30 Min.

**LEADER**

Ask three members of the group, selected ahead of time, to read aloud the Scripture passage. Have one member read the part of Paul; another read the part of Agrippa; and the other read the part of Festus. Ask the whole class to read verses 30–31. Then discuss the Questions for Interaction, dividing into subgroups of four or five.

Certain influential Jews in Jerusalem accused Paul of religious crimes and had him arrested. But since these opponents wanted him dead, they also had to accuse him of civil crimes that Rome would recognize and view as a threat to their rule—creating civil unrest. Read Acts 26:19–32 and see how Paul stands up to these charges.

## Paul Before Agrippa and Festus

Paul: [19]"So then, King Agrippa, I was not disobedient to the vision from heaven. [20]First to those in Damascus, then to those in Jerusalem and in all Judea, and to the Gentiles also, I preached that they should repent and turn to God and prove their repentance by their deeds. [21]That is why the Jews seized me in the temple courts and tried to kill me. [22]But I have had God's help to this very day, and so I stand here and testify to small and great alike. I am saying nothing beyond what the prophets and Moses said would happen—[23]that the Christ would suffer and, as the first to rise from the dead, would proclaim light to his own people and to the Gentiles."

Festus: [24]At this point Festus interrupted Paul's defense. "You are out of your mind, Paul!" he shouted. "Your great learning is driving you insane."

Paul: [25]"I am not insane, most excellent Festus," Paul replied. "What I am saying is true and reasonable. [26]The king is familiar with these things, and I can speak freely to him. I am convinced that none of this has escaped his notice, because it was not done in a corner. [27]King Agrippa, do you believe the prophets? I know you do."

Agrippa: [28]Then Agrippa said to Paul, "Do you think that in such a short time you can persuade me to be a Christian?"

Paul: [29]Paul replied, "Short time or long—I pray God that not only you but all who are listening to me today may become what I am, except for these chains."

Authorities: [30]The king rose, and with him the governor and Bernice and those sitting with them. [31]They left the room, and while talking with one another, they said, "This man is not doing anything that deserves death or imprisonment."

| Agrippa: | [32] *Agrippa said to Festus, "This man could have been set free if he had not appealed to Caesar."* |
|---|---|

*Acts 26:19–32*

## QUESTIONS FOR INTERACTION

**LEADER**

Refer to the Summary and Study Notes at the end of this session. If 30 minutes is not enough time to answer all of the questions in this section, conclude the Bible Study by answering question #7.

1. What was the essence of the message that Paul preached, according to what he said to Agrippa (v. 20)?

2. The teachings of what authorities corroborate Paul's teachings (v. 22)? Why does he take care to refer to these authorities?

3. What seems to be the teaching that prompts Festus to say that Paul is out of his mind? Why might such a teaching have prompted this reaction (see note on v. 24)?

4. What is the significance of the fact that the things Paul talked about were "not done in a corner" (v. 26)?

5. Why does Agrippa feel that Paul is trying to convert him? How does he seem to feel about this? What is Paul's response to this "accusation"?

6. What have you experienced in Christ that you wish everyone you spoke to could truly understand and be a part of?

7. What "chains" do you have on in your life that you would not wish on anyone else?

**GOING DEEPER:** *If your group has time and/or wants a challenge, go on to this next question.*

8. How can a Christian determine when to be bold and direct in his or her faith sharing (v. 29) and when to be more subtle and patient?

# CARING TIME                              15 Min.
## APPLY THE LESSON AND PRAY FOR ONE ANOTHER

**LEADER**

Conclude the group prayer time today by reading Galatians 6:9: *Let us not become weary in doing good, for at the proper time we will reap a harvest if we do not give up.*

This is an important time for you to encourage and support one another in prayer. Take turns sharing your responses to the following questions. Then share prayer requests and close with a group prayer.

1. On a scale of 1 (far apart) to 10 (very close), how closely have you been walking with Jesus this week? What has taken your attention away from him?

2. Have you grown weary in defending your faith? How does Paul's example encourage you not to give up?

3. What help would you like from God in finding release from the "chains" you shared about in question #7?

### NEXT WEEK

Today we heard Paul's unwavering testimony to Agrippa about his faith in Christ. In the coming week, pray daily for a person who seems to be very hard-hearted toward Christ. Also, pray for the opportunity to eventually share your faith with that person. Next week we will see how Paul's ordeal continues as he heads toward trial in Rome, only to be shipwrecked along the way. We will also see how God uses Paul to testify of his power in the midst of that shipwreck.

# NOTES ON ACTS 26:19–32

**Summary:** How would you do if your entire life were put on trial? That is essentially what Paul is experiencing at this point. First he speaks of the early part of his life (26:4–11), and then he speaks of the vision that was instrumental in his conversion (26:12–18). In the section we are looking at in our study, we find the reaction and judgment of Agrippa and Festus to Paul's story. In his presentation Paul seeks to walk a bit of a tightrope. He wants to be respectful and affirming of the authority of Festus and Agrippa, while at the same time boldly proclaiming the truth about Jesus Christ, not wavering from it one iota. Thus he refers to "most excellent Festus" and gives Agrippa the benefit of any doubt in relation to his knowledge of Scripture and what was going on in the world. But he also clearly summarizes the essence of the Gospel of Jesus Christ (vv. 20,23).

The zeal that Paul had for sharing the Gospel is shown in this story perhaps better than anywhere else. Here he is on trial, essentially for his life, and even here his main concern is bringing people to the knowledge of Jesus Christ! As he had shared earlier with lowly jailers (16:29–31), so he now was sharing with the highest officials of the territory, the king and governor of the land. He truly fulfilled his statement in verse 22, "I stand here and testify to small and great alike."

There is some irony in the judgment to which Agrippa and Festus come. Paul had appealed to Caesar because he thought it was necessary to have a chance of regaining his freedom (25:11). Here, however, these two officials make the judgment that if Paul had not appealed to Caesar, they would have set him free. Was this a tragic misstep on Paul's part? It certainly resulted in a longer imprisonment for him, and it may be that he was never free from imprisonment again. But we must remember what the Lord had conveyed to Paul earlier: "As you have testified about me in Jerusalem, so you must also testify in Rome" (23:11). It was through these events that Paul's testimony was brought in a powerful form to the center of the Roman Empire.

**26:19 *King Agrippa.*** The son of Herod Agrippa I (ch. 12). Agrippa II had been appointed as a puppet king (under Roman authority) over some provinces to the northeast of Palestine. *I was not disobedient.* A negative way of expressing Paul's positive eagerness to obey (Rom. 1:15). Implied may be the idea that had he been disobedient to such a vision, there certainly would have been more reason to put him on trial.

**26:20 *in all Judea, and to the Gentiles also.*** Since there is no record of Paul having a ministry in any area of Judea, this might be better understood as his ministry to both Jews and Gentiles in the areas where he traveled. *they should repent and turn to God and prove their repentance by their deeds.* Just as verse 18 sums up the promise of being a Christian, so this verse sums up the conditions required to be a Christian (see also 20:21; Luke 3:8). Faith in Jesus is demonstrated by a lifestyle that reflects a rejection of sin and an embracing of God's ways.

**26:21–23** Although the Jewish hatred of Paul was rooted in his conviction that Gentiles were to be included as the people of God, his message is actually the fulfillment of what the Old Testament had for so long anticipated.

**26:23 the Christ would suffer.** Having made the connection between the Old Testament passages that spoke of the glory of the Messiah with those that spoke of the Suffering Servant of the Lord (Ps. 2; 16; 22; 69; 110; 118; 132; Isa. 11; 42; 49; 53), Paul and the other apostles realized that the suffering and death of Jesus very much fit the pattern of the Old Testament teachings (3:18). **proclaim light to his own people and to the Gentiles.** Paul may have in mind such passages as Genesis 12:3; 22:18; 1 Kings 8:41–43; Psalm 72:8–11; Isaiah 2:3; 45:14,22–25; 49:23; 60:1–3; 65:1 and Malachi 1:11. Paul's point is that his message is most certainly rooted in the Old Testament expectations for the Messiah and should not be the cause of any controversy with the Jews. That there *was* such a controversy was due to the fact that the Jews who chose not to follow Christ probably emphasized other prophecies of the Messiah or interpretations of those prophecies that described a more militaristic and nationalistic type of Messiah.

**26:24** Festus, probably bewildered by Paul's conviction that "a dead man named Jesus" (25:19) was alive and by Paul's talk of a vision that so radically changed his life, broke in with the exasperated cry that Paul must be out of his mind. When Paul taught in Athens, the center of the Greek culture that would have also influenced Festus, it was the mention of the cross and resurrection that turned many of his listeners away scoffing (17:32). Paul also said in 1 Corinthians 1:23 that the cross and resurrection were "foolishness" to Gentiles. However, many in Jewish culture also thought Jesus was crazy (John 10:20), and even Jesus' own family suspected such when he was beginning his ministry (Mark 3:20–21). Jesus had come with such a radically different message than they were expecting, and with such a radically different approach to life, that they saw it as madness.

**26:26 it was not done in a corner.** An idiomatic expression meaning that all Paul has talked about is public knowledge. This might refer to the fact that he had never tried to be secretive about what he taught. It might also refer to the fact that the events of Jesus' life, death and resurrection occurred in Judea, which was at the crossroads of the known world; and hence was not in some obscure place, where the news of the events might not have reached Rome.

**26:27 do you believe the prophets?** The question assumes a "yes" answer. Paul hoped that Agrippa, as a fellow Jew, would acknowledge that there was nothing insane about his belief in the resurrection.

**26:28** This was an attempt at humorous irony. "Christian" was used as a derogatory term at the time, so the humor lay in the (supposedly incongruous) idea of a respected Jewish king being quickly pressed to join forces with a sect other Jews looked down upon.

**26:32 This man could have been set free if he had not appealed to Caesar.** Once an appeal to the emperor had been made, it would have been considered an insult against the emperor and the process of Roman law to short-circuit the process.

# SESSION 11
# SHIPWRECKED

SCRIPTURE   ACTS 27:27–44

**LAST WEEK**

In our last session we saw how Paul testified to his faith in Christ while being tried for his life before Roman authorities. Paul's faithfulness and courage reminded us not to give up on defending our faith. This week we will see how he is taken to Rome to be tried before Caesar and along the way he is shipwrecked. But Paul lets God use him in this also, as he manifests God's power and gives him the glory.

## ICE-BREAKER                                        15 Min.
### CONNECT WITH YOUR GROUP

**LEADER**

Choose one, two or all three Ice-Breaker questions, depending on your group's needs.

We all go through some "storms" in life—some literal and some figurative. Take turns sharing some of your unique life experiences with turbulent times.

1. What is the worst storm you have ever been in? Did you fear for your life? Was there anything that happened during the storm that lightened the tension?

2. If you took all your belongings on board a ship and hit a bad storm, what would be the last thing that you would want to throw overboard?

3. What is the longest you have ever had to go without food? If you had to go without food for a while, what food would you most miss?

# BIBLE STUDY

### READ SCRIPTURE AND DISCUSS

# 30 Min.

**LEADER**

Select a member of the group ahead of time to read the passage. Then discuss the Questions for Interaction, dividing into subgroups of four or five.

Agrippa, about whom we studied about last week, could not make a final decision about Paul's fate because Paul had appealed to Caesar. So Paul was put on a ship to take him to Rome. But the trip was not smooth sailing. Paul advised the centurion in charge that they should stay at a place called Fair Havens until the weather cleared, but the centurion didn't listen. As a result, they ran into a big storm. Read Acts 27:27–44 and take note of how Paul met that storm.

## Paul Shipwrecked

*[27] On the fourteenth night we were still being driven across the Adriatic Sea, when about midnight the sailors sensed they were approaching land. [28] They took soundings and found that the water was a hundred and twenty feet deep. A short time later they took soundings again and found it was ninety feet deep. [29] Fearing that we would be dashed against the rocks, they dropped four anchors from the stern and prayed for daylight. [30] In an attempt to escape from the ship, the sailors let the lifeboat down into the sea, pretending they were going to lower some anchors from the bow. [31] Then Paul said to the centurion and the soldiers, "Unless these men stay with the ship, you cannot be saved." [32] So the soldiers cut the ropes that held the lifeboat and let it fall away.*

*[33] Just before dawn Paul urged them all to eat. "For the last fourteen days," he said, "you have been in constant suspense and have gone without food—you haven't eaten anything. [34] Now I urge you to take some food. You need it to survive. Not one of you will lose a single hair from his head." [35] After he said this, he took some bread and gave thanks to God in front of them all. Then he broke it and began to eat. [36] They were all encouraged and ate some food themselves.*

*[37] Altogether there were 276 of us on board. [38] When they had eaten as much as they wanted, they lightened the ship by throwing the grain into the sea.*

*[39] When daylight came, they did not recognize the land, but they saw a bay with a sandy beach, where they decided to run the ship aground if they could. [40] Cutting loose the anchors, they left them in the sea and at the same time untied the ropes that held the rudders. Then they hoisted the foresail to the wind and made for the beach. [41] But the ship struck a sandbar and ran aground. The bow stuck fast and would not move, and the stern was broken to pieces by the pounding of the surf.*

*[42] The soldiers planned to kill the prisoners to prevent any of them from swimming away and escaping. [43] But the centurion*

*wanted to spare Paul's life and kept them from carrying out their plan. He ordered those who could swim to jump overboard first and get to land. ⁴⁴The rest were to get there on planks or on pieces of the ship. In this way everyone reached land in safety.*

*Acts 27:27–44*

## QUESTIONS FOR INTERACTION

**LEADER**

Refer to the Summary and Study Notes at the conclusion of this session. If 30 minutes is not enough time to answer all of the questions in this section, conclude the Bible Study by answering question #7.

1. Had you been on this ship with Paul, what aspect of the experience would have been hardest for you?
   ❐ Going without food for so long.
   ❐ The tossing of the ship (which would have kept you from keeping down food anyway).
   ❐ Fear of dying.
   ❐ All the tension between people whose nerves were strained.
   ❐ Other _____.

2. What signs do the sailors find that indicate they are approaching land (see vv. 27–28 and note for v. 27)? What feelings do you think those on board were experiencing at this point?

3. What do the sailors try to do in order to "save their own skins"? What does Paul do to keep this from happening?

4. What is the attitude of those on board toward what Paul says at this point? Why do you think they were willing to give him so much credence (see for comparison 27:9–12)? What is the most effective thing Paul does to inspire their confidence?

5. Who saves Paul from being executed? Why do you think he did so?
   ❐ Out of respect.
   ❐ Because he had seen the quality of Paul's leadership and felt he was needed.
   ❐ Other _____.

6. Paul conveyed a promise of God that all would survive. What promise of God are you relying on right now in your life? What would you say is your level of confidence in that promise?
   ❐ Fully assured.
   ❐ Mostly confident.
   ❐ Sort of "iffy."
   ❐ Actually, running scared.

**7.** What storm are you experiencing right now in your life? What "signs of land" do you see that give you hope?

**GOING DEEPER:** *If your group has time and/or wants a challenge, go on to this next question.*

**8.** When you sense that the church you are part of is a "sinking ship," when do you "abandon ship" and go find another church, and when do you say, "We have to all stick together to make it through this"?

# CARING TIME                    15 Min.
## APPLY THE LESSON AND PRAY FOR ONE ANOTHER

. . . . . . . . . . . . . . . . . . . . . . . . . . . . . . . . . . . . . . . . . . . . .

**LEADER**

Conclude the prayer time by asking God for guidance in determining the future mission and outreach of this group.

Paul encouraged his fellow sailors and gave them hope. Take some time now to encourage and support one another with a time of sharing and prayer.

**1.** How has God been at work in your life this past week?

**2.** When have you felt "shipwrecked" emotionally or physically? How did God deliver you?

**3.** What encouragement can you give the other members of your group in the midst of the storms they shared about in question #7? Take time for everyone to share such a word of encouragement for the person on his or her right.

### NEXT WEEK

Today we saw how Paul remained calm in the midst of a terrible storm as he relied on God's promises. This helped all of those around him to also remain calm and see the power of God at work. In the coming week, memorize one of God's promises that will help you amidst the storms of your life (e.g., Matt. 11:28; Phil. 4:13). Next week we will see how those on board the ship make it to an island called Malta, and how Paul once again manifests God's presence and power.

# NOTES ON ACTS 27:27–44

**Summary:** A person's character comes out most clearly not when life is "smooth sailing," but when one is facing a storm. In a furious storm, Jesus remained calm and collected while his disciples panicked (Matt. 8:23–27). In a violent storm, Jonah's weakness was discerned (Jonah 1:1–17). And here in a shipwreck Paul is seen to be a leader who gives firm leadership because he depends on the promises of God. He kept together all of those persons whose skills were necessary for survival (v. 31), and he led by both word and example in getting those on board to eat what they needed for strength, and trust a promise from God that they would all survive (vv. 33–36).

Paul was able to remain strong and confident in this storm because he had learned how to do so in a life full of storms. In the course of his ministry, even before this moment, by his report: "Five times I received from the Jews the forty lashes minus one. Three times I was beaten with rods, once I was stoned, three times I was shipwrecked [before this time!], I spent a night and day in the open sea, I have been constantly on the move. I have been in danger from rivers, in danger from bandits, in danger from my own countrymen, in danger from Gentiles; in danger in the city, in danger in the country, in danger at sea; and in danger from false brothers. I have labored and toiled and have often gone without sleep; I have known hunger and thirst and have often gone without food; I have been cold and naked" (2 Cor. 11:24–27). And of course all of this didn't stop after this particular shipwreck. He was imprisoned for a couple of years in Rome. From there he wrote letters showing his continued resolve under this kind of "storm." He wrote the Philippians from jail, "I have learned to be content whatever the circumstances" (Phil. 4:11). And he called upon them to "Rejoice in the Lord always" (Phil. 4:4).

In the midst of these storms, it's important for us to acknowledge that it was not the natural strength of Paul's character that helped him through them, but rather strength from God. Here in this story, the key to Paul's strength is his faith in the promise of God that he would survive the storm, along with all of the others (v. 34), and that he would testify on Christ's behalf in Rome (23:11). Later Paul wrote, again in Philippians, "I can do everything through him who gives me strength" (Phil. 4:13). So when we go through storms our response should not be, "But I'm not strong like Paul," but rather, realizing that we have the same God and the same Christ, we can say with Paul, "I can do everything through him who gives me strength."

**27:27 On the fourteenth night.** Presumably from the time they left Fair Havens. **the Adriatic Sea.** While this term today only applies to the body of water between Italy and the Balkans, in Paul's day it included the sea between Sicily and Crete. **sensed they were approaching land.** Probably by hearing the waves break on the coast.

**27:29 they dropped four anchors from the stern.** If anchors had been dropped from the bow (which was the usual practice) the ship would have swung around and been facing the wrong way to attempt a beaching on shore in the morning.

**27:30–32** At least some of the sailors apparently had had enough of the ship. Concerned only with getting to shore as soon as possible, they planned to make a run for shore on their own that night under pretense of securing the ship. How Paul knew their real intention is not mentioned. However, he is concerned that the rest of the passengers' safety depends upon the experience of the sailors. This time, the centurion does not hesitate to act on Paul's warning! Why the sailors would leave the safety of the ship to attempt a nighttime landing in a stormy sea on an unknown shore can only be attributed to panic and exhaustion.

**27:33–36** Once again Paul takes the lead to encourage the passengers. The description of his eating is similar to that used to describe the Lord's Supper (1 Cor. 11:23–24), but it is most likely that he simply followed the Jewish and Christian custom of offering thanks to God for his food and proceeded to eat as an example to the others. This action may also have indicated his assurance that the danger was now past and that God indeed had answered his prayers.

**27:37 *there were 276 of us.*** Luke probably mentions this to point out the greatness of the miracle that not one of such a large number was lost in such a severe storm.

**27:38 *throwing the grain into the sea.*** Previously, all portable cargo was jettisoned (v. 18), but now the main load itself was removed to lighten the ship as much as possible so that it might have the best possible chance of making it to shore.

**27:39–40** In the morning, the crew decided to head for a sandy beach. The anchors were cut away, the steering oars (which had been lashed up overnight) were set in operation, and the foresail raised so they could make a run for shore.

**27:41** Instead, the ship ran aground on an unseen sandbar. The traditional site of St. Paul's Bay on the island of Malta is composed of mud and clay, which would trap a ship stuck in it. The pounding of the waves soon began to break the ship apart.

**27:42–43** Since the soldiers were responsible for making sure prisoners did not escape in transit, some of the soldiers planned to kill the prisoners on the spot rather than face the possibility that some might escape in the chaos. Because of the centurion's respect for Paul, he prevented that action from happening. Instead, he ordered everyone to abandon ship and make it to shore as best they could.

**27:44 *on pieces of the ship.*** The Greek is ambiguous allowing the phrase to be translated as "on things from the ship" or "on people from the ship." Those who could swim were probably involved in helping those who could not to shore. In this way, Paul's prophecy was fulfilled (27:24).

# SESSION 12
# ASHORE ON MALTA

SCRIPTURE   ACTS 28:1–10

## LAST WEEK

Last week we looked at the shipwreck that occurred when Paul was being transported to Rome for trial before Caesar. Even in this extreme situation, Paul remained calm and relied on God's promises. This week we will see the continuation of that story as Paul and his shipmates are stranded on the island of Malta. Here, once again, God will show his mighty works through Paul, this time through his miraculous recovery from a deadly snakebite and many healings.

## ICE-BREAKER                                          15 Min.
### CONNECT WITH YOUR GROUP

**LEADER**

Choose one, two or all three of the Ice-Breaker questions, depending on your group's needs.

Paul was a survivor. He survived many things that might have killed him, including a shipwreck and snakebite. Take turns sharing your experiences with tough circumstances or circumstances where you needed the assistance of others.

1.  If you were to get stranded on an island, with whom would you most want to be stranded? What one thing would you most want to have with you in your "survival kit"?

2.  What is the worst disaster or illness you have had to survive? Who or what helped you the most during this time?

3.  What out-of-town friend or family member can you most count on to show you hospitality? What do you enjoy doing when you stay with this person?

# BIBLE STUDY

## READ SCRIPTURE AND DISCUSS

# 30 Min.

**LEADER**

Select a member of the group ahead of time to read the Scripture passage. Then discuss the Questions for Interaction, dividing into subgroups of four or five.

*Castaway* with Tom Hanks was a popular movie about a man stranded on an island. In our passage for today, Paul has his own "Castaway" experience, except that he shares it with a number of other people, instead of with a volleyball named "Wilson." While Hank's character learned what he was made of, in this case the other people learned what Paul was made of—a tremendous faith and courage from God. Read Acts 28:1–10 and take note of how Paul ministers to others.

### Ashore on Malta

**28** *Once safely on shore, we found out that the island was called Malta.* ²*The islanders showed us unusual kindness. They built a fire and welcomed us all because it was raining and cold.* ³*Paul gathered a pile of brushwood and, as he put it on the fire, a viper, driven out by the heat, fastened itself on his hand.* ⁴*When the islanders saw the snake hanging from his hand, they said to each other, "This man must be a murderer; for though he escaped from the sea, Justice has not allowed him to live."* ⁵*But Paul shook the snake off into the fire and suffered no ill effects.* ⁶*The people expected him to swell up or suddenly fall dead, but after waiting a long time and seeing nothing unusual happen to him, they changed their minds and said he was a god.*

⁷*There was an estate nearby that belonged to Publius, the chief official of the island. He welcomed us to his home and for three days entertained us hospitably.* ⁸*His father was sick in bed, suffering from fever and dysentery. Paul went in to see him and, after prayer, placed his hands on him and healed him.* ⁹*When this had happened, the rest of the sick on the island came and were cured.* ¹⁰*They honored us in many ways and when we were ready to sail, they furnished us with the supplies we needed.*

*Acts 28:1–10*

**LEADER**

Refer to the Summary and Study Notes at the end of this session. If 30 minutes is not enough time to answer all of the questions in this section, conclude the Bible Study by answering question #7.

## QUESTIONS FOR INTERACTION

**1.** What is your fondest memory of gathering with people around a warm fire and what made it memorable?
❑ Summer camp as a kid.
❑ A family camping trip.
❑ In a lodge after skiing.
❑ Other _____.

**2.** What does it show you about the people of Malta that they were willing to show hospitality to a group that included prisoners in transport? Do you think the people of your church would have shown the same kind of hospitality? Why or why not?

**3.** What does Paul's miraculous resistance to this snakebite show about God's presence with him and God's plan for him (look again at 23:11)?

**4.** How does the attitude of the islanders toward Paul change during the course of this passage? What events influence this change?

**5.** How do you think Paul felt about being regarded as a god? When had this happened previously and how did Paul react (Acts 14:8–18)? What effect did it probably have on this attitude when Paul started healing people?

**6.** What "venom" do you most need God's protection from right now?
❐ The venom of hatred that certain people have toward you.
❐ The venom of your own bitterness or guilt.
❐ The venom of financial hardship.
❐ The venom of physical disease.
❐ Other _____.

To what degree are you confident that God can pull you through your "snakebite"?

**7.** In what specific ways can you emulate Paul—ministering to others while heading toward your own somewhat frightening future?

**GOING DEEPER:** *If your group has time and/or wants a challenge, go on to this next question.*

**8.** What does it say about Paul that he was ministering to others in this way while on his way to being put on trial for his life? To what degree were his actions the result of his natural character, and to what degree were they the result of God working in him?

# CARING TIME                              15 Min.
## APPLY THE LESSON AND PRAY FOR ONE ANOTHER

**LEADER**

Following the Caring Time, discuss with your group how they would like to celebrate the last session next week. Also, discuss the possibility of splitting into two groups and continuing with another study.

In today's Scripture passage, Paul's prayers brought great healing to many people. Take some time now to encourage and support one another with a time of sharing and prayer.

1. What challenge are you facing this week or in the near future?

2. In what area of your life do you most need God's healing touch right now?

3. What help do you need from God to minister in the way you talked about in question #7?

---

**NEXT WEEK**

This week we saw God working through Paul even after he was shipwrecked and stranded on an island. In the coming week, pray that God would use all of your difficult circumstances for his glory. In our next and final session we will look at what happens when Paul goes on to Rome, and we will consider the possible conclusion to his life story that Acts does not tell about.

# NOTES ON ACTS 28:1–10

**Summary:** When we look back at the people of history who are most credited with influencing the major advances in our world, it's often a temptation to see them as more than human. We think, surely they were not like us! Surely they didn't have our weaknesses, our foibles. Surely they always had the right word for the right time, and when you looked at them, there was probably a visible glow around them. George Washington, Shakespeare and Beethoven—didn't they always have a dignity and perfection that made them seem cast in marble? Some of us might think of the apostle Paul that way, and if we do, this story probably only accentuates the tendency. Not only did he have the bravery and vision to see the ship he was on through a shipwreck, but he also shook off the poison of a deadly viper as if it were just a mosquito bite. Then, instead of being deathly ill himself, he went on to cure the father of an important official. How could a person who did these things be at all like us? We may even empathize a little with those who at the time mistook him for a god (v. 6).

Instead of thinking of Paul as being so great, we need to look at the greatness of the God who worked through him in this way. After all, this was still the man who started off persecuting Christians, and who sometimes lost his temper at inappropriate times (23:2–5). The God of Jesus Christ is the one who took this imperfect person and made him into one who could do great wonders. The God of Jesus Christ was also the one who took the Peter who denied Christ and changed him into the Peter who was the "rock" on which Christ built his church. And this same God can do similar wonders with us if we let him.

**28:1–10** The ship's crew had landed at Malta, a small island 60 miles to the south of Sicily. The Phoenicians had long before settled Malta, and their influence was still heard in the language of the people.

**28:2** *The islanders.* Literally, "the barbarians." This term was used when referring to someone who did not speak Greek. *built a fire.* Since there were 276 survivors, probably several fires were built around which small groups huddled. Luke focuses in on the one that affected him and Paul.

**28:3** *gathered a pile of brushwood.* Paul was not so "spiritual" that he was above doing the physical work necessary for the common good. *a viper.* There are no poisonous snakes on Malta today, but the ecology may have been different in Paul's time. The onlookers certainly regarded this snake as poisonous.

**28:4** *This man must be a murderer.* Like many societies, these people felt that hardship was the result of divine punishment for some sin. While the book of Job had questioned this in Old Testament times, it was still a common way of thinking in Jewish society as well as Greek. Jesus denied that a person who experiences hardship or tragedy is necessarily a worse sinner than anyone else (Luke 13:1–5). *Justice.* Literally, "Dike." This was the name for the Greek goddess of Justice, one of the daughters of Zeus. *has not allowed him to live.* Paul, who had been spared from such a disaster as a shipwreck only to be bitten by a viper, must have certainly committed a serious crime for which the gods will not allow him to escape.

**28:6** *he was a god.* Although Luke says nothing about this, it is inconceivable that Paul would allow such an opinion to stand once he became aware of it (14:11–18). Paul undoubtedly used the next three months to dissuade the people from that belief and to persuade them to put their hope in Jesus.

**28:7 *the chief official of the island.*** The exact Greek word, *protos,* has been found in two inscriptions as a title of an official on Malta, showing the accuracy of Luke in recording this detail. It is unclear whether this was a native official or the representative of the Roman authority on Malta.

**28:8 *placed his hands on him and healed him.*** Miraculous healing most commonly involved this kind of touch (9:12,17), because such healing came through the Holy Spirit and the Holy Spirit was conveyed by placing hands on a person (6:6; 8:17; 13:3; 19:6).

# SESSION 13
# AN IRREPRESSIBLE BOLDNESS

SCRIPTURE   ACTS 28:16–31

## LAST WEEK

Paul's witness when stranded on the island of Malta inspired us in last week's session. This week his witness takes a larger, more influential stage as he moves on to Rome, the heart of the ancient world. There he maintained a vital ministry, even while in prison, that has guided and touched Christians down through the centuries.

## ICE-BREAKER                                   15 Min.
### CONNECT WITH YOUR GROUP

**LEADER**

Begin this final session with a word of prayer and thanksgiving for this time together. Choose one or two Ice-Breaker questions to discuss.

Paul's troubles with the "powers that be" brought him to Rome as a prisoner. Take turns sharing your own experiences with authority figures.

1.  Finish this sentence: "The most trouble I have been in with the law was when ..."

2.  When in your life have you most felt like you were "under guard"?
    ❏ When you lived with your parents as a teen.
    ❏ When in the armed forces.
    ❏ When you started a new job.
    ❏ Other _____.

3.  If you were called before a group of people to defend how you have lived your life, what would you say?

# BIBLE STUDY

### READ SCRIPTURE AND DISCUSS

# 30 Min.

## LEADER

Select two members of the group ahead of time to read aloud the passage. Have one member read Luke's narration, and the other read the part of Paul. Ask the whole class to read the part of the Jewish leaders. Then discuss the Questions for Interaction, dividing into subgroups of four or five.

People who can't wait to see how a story turns out often go right to the end of the book. Unfortunately, people who do that with Acts might be somewhat disappointed. There is much we don't know about how things turned out for Paul. But in another sense, we learn in this closing story all the essentials—his witness to Jesus Christ remained strong to the end! Read Acts 28:16–31 and note Paul's final words to the Jewish leaders.

## Paul Preaches at Rome Under Guard

Luke: *<sup>16</sup>When we got to Rome, Paul was allowed to live by himself, with a soldier to guard him. <sup>17</sup>Three days later he called together the leaders of the Jews. When they had assembled, Paul said to them:*

Paul: *"My brothers, although I have done nothing against our people or against the customs of our ancestors, I was arrested in Jerusalem and handed over to the Romans. <sup>18</sup>They examined me and wanted to release me, because I was not guilty of any crime deserving death. <sup>19</sup>But when the Jews objected, I was compelled to appeal to Caesar—not that I had any charge to bring against my own people. <sup>20</sup>For this reason I have asked to see you and talk with you. It is because of the hope of Israel that I am bound with this chain."*

Leaders: *<sup>21</sup>They replied, "We have not received any letters from Judea concerning you, and none of the brothers who have come from there has reported or said anything bad about you. <sup>22</sup>But we want to hear what your views are, for we know that people everywhere are talking against this sect."*

Luke: *<sup>23</sup>They arranged to meet Paul on a certain day, and came in even larger numbers to the place where he was staying. From morning till evening he explained and declared to them the kingdom of God and tried to convince them about Jesus from the Law of Moses and from the Prophets. <sup>24</sup>Some were convinced by what he said, but others would not believe. <sup>25</sup>They disagreed among themselves and began to leave after Paul had made this final statement:*

Paul: *"The Holy Spirit spoke the truth to your forefathers when he said through Isaiah the prophet:*
*<sup>26</sup>'Go to this people and say,*
*"You will be ever hearing but never understanding;*
*you will be ever seeing but never perceiving."*

*27For this people's heart has become calloused;*
*they hardly hear with their ears*
*and they have closed their eyes.*
*Otherwise they might see with their eyes*
*hear with their ears,*
*understand with their hearts*
*and turn, and I would heal them.'*
   *28"Therefore I want you to know that God's salvation has been sent to the Gentiles, and they will listen!"*

Luke:      *30For two whole years Paul stayed there in his own rented house and welcomed all who came to see him. 31Boldly and without hindrance he preached the kingdom of God and taught about the Lord Jesus Christ.*

*Acts 28:16–31*

## LEADER

Refer to the Summary and Study Notes at the conclusion of this session as needed. If 30 minutes is not enough time to answer all the questions in this section, conclude the Bible Study by answering question #7.

## QUESTIONS FOR INTERACTION

**1.** Who seems to "hardly hear with their ears" when you speak to them?
❒ Your children.
❒ Your spouse.
❒ Your boss.
❒ The government.
❒ A business complaint department.
❒ Other _____.

**2.** How would you describe Paul as you see him in this last story of Acts?

**3.** What would you say seems to be Paul's main concern in this passage?

**4.** Why does Paul say he is bound in chains?

**5.** What would you see as the most influential factor in Paul being able to preach the Gospel boldly while under arrest?

**6.** Were you to share your faith more boldly, where would your main opposition come from?

**7.** Were you to share your faith more boldly, where would you start? What kind of help or support would you need?

# NOTES ON ACTS 28:16–31

. . . . . . . . . . . . . . . . . . . . . . . . . . . . . . . . . . . . . . . . . . . . . . . . . .

**Summary:** In the book of Acts there is a consistent connection between the presence of the Holy Spirit and the boldness with which the disciples acted. The words "boldly" and "boldness" or their equivalent are used eight different times in the Book of Acts: 4:13; 4:29; 4:31; 9:27–28; 13:46; 14:3; 18:26; 19:8. To understand our passage it might be best to first look at 4:13. It says there, "Now when they [the Sanhedrin, a kind of Jewish Supreme Court] saw the boldness of Peter and John and realized that they were uneducated and ordinary men, they were amazed and recognized them as companions of Jesus" (NRSV). What is the connection between the first phrase of this sentence and the second? Boldness and (probably) eloquence did not go together in the minds of these educated religious leaders with "uneducated and ordinary men." This started them thinking, "In what other person have we seen this behavior?" Immediately they thought of Jesus the prophet from Nazareth. Boldness was a mark of having been with Christ. When you think about it, that is a natural reaction. When you realize that even death can't defeat you, isn't it natural to be bold?

Paul had been arrested in Jerusalem and transferred to prison in Rome. In verse 16 we learn of the conditions under which he lived. At first he was given a fair amount of freedom. Basically, he was under house arrest. This freedom is what allowed him to write the letters he wrote while a prisoner in Rome. These include Ephesians (Eph. 4:1; 6:19–20); Philippians (Phil. 1:7, 12–14,19–26); Colossians (Col. 4:3–4,18); and Philemon (Philem. 1,9,13). Philippians 1:12–13 gives an insight to his situation during this time as he carried on an extensive ministry to the soldiers assigned to guard him, undoubtedly resulting in the conversion of a number of them.

**28:16 *Paul was allowed to live by himself.*** Paul was not kept in a prison, but kept under guard in a type of house arrest while he awaited trial. He may have been able to work as a leather-worker during this time, or gifts from the churches that cared for him may have provided for his needs (Phil. 4:14–18).

**28:17–22** As soon as possible, Paul called together the leaders of the synagogues in Rome (at least 13 are known to have existed). He held this meeting in order to explain his situation to them first-hand so they might not be influenced more by rumors than personal information.

**28:19 *my own people.*** Notice also "my brothers" and "our ancestors" (v. 17). Once again, Luke presents Paul as a faithful Jew;

his commitment to Jesus as the Messiah is to be seen as a natural outgrowth of his trust in the Old Testament Scriptures and his loyalty to God (v. 20; 23:6; 24:15; 26:22–23). His appeal to Caesar is not to be construed as trying to bring any problems to the Jews either in Rome or Jerusalem.

**28:22 *people everywhere are talking about this sect.*** A church had been established among the Jewish community in Rome for at least 20 years and perhaps as far back as Pentecost nearly 30 years earlier (2:10). Paul's letter to Rome, written about three years before his arrival, deals extensively with conflicts arising between Jewish and Gentile elements in the church there. Thus, these Jewish leaders certainly knew something of Christianity, but they may have desired to finally get some answers to questions that had never been clearly explained to them.

**28:23** Examples of how Paul argued for the Gospel from the Old Testament Scriptures are given in 13:16–41; 22:3–21 and 26:4–27. **the kingdom of God.** Throughout the Gospels, the message of Jesus is known as the message of the kingdom of God (Mark 1:15). This phrase serves as summary of what the entire Gospel is about—it announces the present and coming reign of God in human affairs and calls people to affirm their loyalty to Jesus as God's appointed king.

**28:25–27** Paul accounts for the unbelief of many through the words of the prophet Isaiah in Isaiah 6:9–10 (see also Mark 4:12). In its context, this passage spoke of the fact that although God sent Isaiah to call Israel to repent, the net effect of his preaching would be that people would become even more hardened against God. Verse 27 is full of a sad irony: it is as if the people deliberately block their ears and shut their eyes to God as though the last thing they want is to turn to God and be forgiven. By quoting this passage, Paul is calling on his Jewish hearers not to follow in the footsteps of their forefathers who rejected Isaiah and his message.

**28:30** Luke concludes Acts with the picture of Paul continuing his missionary activities with all who would listen. **his own rented house.** See note on 28:16.

**28:31** In this last statement in Acts, the emphasis in the Greek sentence falls on the boldness and freedom with which Paul preached the Gospel. During this period of house arrest, Paul wrote the letter of Philippians and probably the letters of Ephesians, Colossians and Philemon as well. While some believe that at the end of these two years Paul was executed, other scholars contend that Paul was released and enjoyed freedom for another two years, during which he traveled once again to Crete, Asia and Macedonia. It was during this time that it is believed he wrote the letters of 1 Timothy and Titus. According to this second perspective, at some point after this, he was again arrested and imprisoned at Rome, but this time things were far more sinister. The Emperor Nero, widely suspected of having started the great fire of Rome in A.D. 64, needed to shift the blame off of himself onto someone else and Christians were chosen as the culprits. This resulted in an outburst of cruel persecution against the church during which it is believed both Paul and Peter were executed by Roman authorities.

PS 22:3 But you are holy - you that inhabit the praises of isniel.

worship isn't = to music

Its amazing how we can have a lack of passion for God And it cant effect His passion for us. And the H.S. still drives us sometimes when we are total unaware - And so we end up in church wondering why we dont feel the way Bob encouraged us to. (as other Bob or Pastor Doug) Good to know you can still praise God + Come to the place where His spirit can have an even greater effect on us.

Epe 5:20 Priority List
1 Tm 4:2 conscience ceared w/hot iron

# Personal Notes

- ministry time - like an inner shower. If you could smell
  your inner man - you would run to the alter...

we need to ask f/ a Revival of wanting c/o God.
which will lead to a impartation of [anruih]tion
but it'z birthed here in prayer + ministry time

- my testimony about ministry time wh? evey week.
why so needy -
we need to be wanty - wanty God.
we all have needs only God can provide
but it'z when we are wanting + needing of God
that those things get closer.
could we be as needy for you as we know we are
without you.
Not everyones verdect is like Mshak Shadrack
+ Winabego

- not every one is freed from teqrip of the
enemy because of they're Righeooship.

Not everyones pardon is to do in my part

reseting is equipping (Greek picture)

sometimes God has to break us to release

perception will determine your conception
(I perceive you a Holy man)

Its in us (the kingdom) but we have to apply it.
assume ownership of it + put it into [practice]
View the end not the moment (despising not the shame
Jesus didn't die for me but as me] He for the joy
which is why I still have to die      Soul
not to be saved      Body      spirit      mind
will

Rachel/Dawn

not just to me, Lord but through me - pouring out

church says too often - what people aren't rather than build them up by telling them who they are.

Jealosy cant effect you unless you are willing to doubt your self worth but it also works both ways.

God allows some people from they're problem not because of they're rightousness but because hes not done w/ them (He sees promise in)

If I didn't feel like getting up this morning passionate for Jesus + church (I still got here) because the power in me is greater + knows what I feel. I envited that spirit now it deals w/me ⟨Im natural is our problem not even you can feed a child ... but not a mature adult⟩

2 Tim 1:12 I sufer but am not ashamed, when paul sofered he didn't feel shame.

"Shame on you" was that ever said

Mat 22:37 2 favorite comandments our self image will reflect how we relate to others. You cant really give what you have. (we dont realy love ourselves) which is why we give into shame + fail to mature -

shame has a voice - Does that voice belong to
someone in your life (you now

# Personal Notes

Anointing that will last + have great
effect will come out.

out pouring vs. pouring out
Anointing that falls on the flesh is limited
cross confounds the mind - memories -
abuse confounds the mind meditations -
                                              thoughts.
Jesus despised shame - Rejected it.
cycle - syndrome (shame) don't measure up.
If they're shame in you how can you manafest
the kingdom. This makes you codependant beleivs?
Your begging God or chasing anointing of God
in other ministrs to get a washing
of Rx - just for today. Its not being
released from Christ within.

pouring out (mind set on the flesh is sin)
when jesus went to the cross + didnt despise
the shame, if He beleive the lie -
" Physician Heal yourself, get off the cross"
shame was put on him - But while he
despised it He bore sin
shame is a feely -        over       Rom 10  who ever
Its a feely I'm not enough       beleivs will not be
                                                  ashamed
   Is 54:4      Syndrome of not being Good enough
(To feel not enough)

Is your soul lord over your spirit   (maturety)
Paul " I would like to bring you meat
1Cor 3:2    shame is an attack on who you are (deeper)
Guilt is about what you do or dont do
excessive Guilt is Condemnation

noah - 4    Liz    (Lifter of thy head)
zecuria - 0
Elizabeth
Mighty through God for pulling down strongholds - dispose shame

# Personal Notes

not Shame
We should be filled w/ Glory not shame
we can worship dance, take note but is it filled w/ shame or Glory

The fathers blessing - Love of the father will

be to the sons + sons to the fathers

We must give oil away.

Can we be satisfied by seeing our father

on weekends. Are you the one who

knew a father of weekends only.

Is it hard for you to think your

father in heaven would make you his

9-5 Routine. Are you Fathering on your own
with nothing but what you figured out since you were a kid.
own because you think you haven't ANY

role to this time until Sunday.

or worse have you substituted Sunday

as a compromise because - your natural

father was totally or almost totally absent

Shame has a voice
① secular culture - look good, make good.
② graceless Religion - works, customs, outside oriented ( Roots say of shame)
③ ungraceful parents / our destiny has a voice to inspirt in Christ

**GOING DEEPER:** *If your group has time and/or wants a challenge, go on to this next question.*

8. Are there ways of witnessing for Christ that make it more likely the listener's heart will become "calloused" (v. 27)? Are there ways a Christian can witness that would make it less likely the listener's heart will become calloused or hardened?

# CARING TIME                    15 Min.
## APPLY THE LESSON AND PRAY FOR ONE ANOTHER

**LEADER**

Conclude this final Caring Time by praying for each group member and asking for God's blessing in any plans to start a new group and/or continue to study together.

Gather around each other now in this final time of sharing and prayer and give each other the strength to go out and "boldly and without hindrance" (v. 31) share Christ with others.

1. What have you gained from this study of Acts (chapters 15–28)? Which of Paul's characteristics would you like to incorporate more into your life?

2. What continuing support do you need in order to maintain the bold witness we read about in this last chapter of Acts?

3. What will you remember most about this group? How would you like the group to continue to pray for you?